To Beverly
Best Wishes!

Oct 5, 1909

THE RUSSIANS: VICTIMS OF HISTORY

THE RUSSIANS:
Victims of history

From Yaroslavl to Yeltsin

David B. Stenzel, Ph. D.

The Book Guild Ltd
Sussex, England

The Book Guild Ltd
25 High Street,
Lewes, Sussex

First published 1997
© David B. Stenzel
Set in Times
Typesetting by Raven Typesetters, Chester
Printed in Great Britain by
Bookcraft (Bath) Ltd,
Avon

A catalogue record for this book is
available from the British Library

ISBN 1 85776 286 X

To Muriel with whom I have sailed the seas of matrimonial bliss for nearly 40 years

CONTENTS

1

INTRODUCTION

Russia has always baffled Americans as well as most Western
Europeans, despite a closer proximity to the giant. How can the
people of a land with such great potential have suffered such a tragic
history characterized by periodic catastrophes? During centuries of
oppression the country flipped from one despotism to another. Its
immense possibilities for economic growth have been constantly
stifled by a succession of barbaric periods in its history. How can
this have come about? The nation cannot be understood by the West
and remains impenetrable. Winston Churchill once said that Russia
is a "riddle, wrapped in a mystery, inside an enigma". Implausible
though it seems, that, at least, is the beginning of an insight into the
West's problem with Russia. The traditional understanding of history in which a people struggle to create a separate identity and
develop the self-government that leads to nationhood cannot be
applied to Russia. Its monstrous history makes rational analysis
almost impossible, but we can try. However, the last half of the 20th
century shows that further informed insights, even along the lines of
Churchill's, have been in short supply.

As the Cold War intensified, American Intelligence was caught
off-guard. Hardly anyone in America understood Russian. All the
American foreign policy experts, with a few exceptions, had
majored in French or Spanish, or German, rather than Russian.
For this reason the American Intelligence community had to rely
heavily upon refugee scholars from Eastern Europe whose conservative views did much to bias American policy against the
Russians.

Why has Russia remained so unknown in the West? I can suggest three major reasons. First, Russia is not a charter member of Western civilization. She received her Christianity from Constantinople, not from Rome. This meant that she absorbed a Graeco-Oriental culture, not a Latin-Germanic one as we did in the West. Her art, architecture, music and general character all reflect this accident of historical geography.

Second, early in her history, Russia was conquered by the Mongols, a conquest so ruthless and thorough that it cut Russia off from Western contacts for several centuries. The military control by the Mongols lasted 200 years from 1237 to 1480, and their cultural yoke another two centuries, really until the beginning of the 18th century. So for over 400 years Russia missed out on the economic and cultural revival that was propelling Western Europe toward the modern world. This meant that Russia was behind the West and would be overcome by a passion to catch up with the West, a passion that has lasted for centuries.

A third reason for Western ignorance of Russia is because of the veil of paranoia erected by the Bolsheviks after 1917. The Bolsheviks wanted only minimal contact with the outside world, which they considered a collection of capitalist enemies.

For all these reasons, Russia developed differently from the West and has been considered a cultural outsider ever since her people were first introduced to the West in the early 18th century after a 400-year separation.

There are, nevertheless, some striking similarities between Russia and America. Both are huge nations. Both enjoy a frontier psychology (Americans went West, they went East) that was formed by a similar historical sequence of hunters followed by farmers, followed by towns, and now by McDonalds. Both nations enjoy a cultural mix – Russia being European and Asian; America being primarily European and African.

Both are relatively new nations and started about the same time. Russia began to emerge as a free nation after 1462, just before Colombus stumbled on America on his way to Japan. Russia became involved with world politics with Peter the Great in the 18th century just before the United States was born.

But there are also striking contrasts between Russia and

America. First, Russians have suffered an appalling lack of security. They have been subject to frequent, sudden, devastating invasions over the centuries. Many of these have come from Asia with one frightening wave of barbarians after another ravaging the land. Evidence of this can be seen in the many fortified monasteries built to withstand attack as well as to extend the Gospel. There remains even today a latent fear of Asians, most recently manifested by tension between Russia and China.

Russia has also been subject to frequent invasions from Europe. The city of Smolensk, for example, has been destroyed 21 times so far in its history (seriously affecting real-estate values). And the memories of the devastation of World War II have never faded. Even today bridal parties will go to a World War II monument to exchange toasts and good wishes.

The roster of invaders of Russia is a frightening one: Scythians, Avars, Djungars, Goths, Huns, Khazars, Black Bolgars, Mongols, Tatars, Swedes, Lithuanians, Poles, French, Germans, and now tourists.

The United States has faced no such fearsome enemies. There is the happy insulation of two oceans, which gives it time to plan and prepare for war. America does not cower in fear of an attack by Cuba or Venezuela. No power can play balance-of-power in this hemisphere because no country can hope to match the might of America. If America goes to war, it has at least a year to study the training manuals ("So you are going to have a war?"), train an army, equip and supply it, recruit Hollywood stars to entertain the troops, etc. Russia never had such a luxury of time.

Russia has also suffered from centuries of suppression under the Mongols, the Tsars, and the Communists. They have no democratic tradition, whereas in the American haven of individual freedom "Anything Goes".

Geography has also played a crucial role in molding the Russian character and directing her history. Russia is a vast flat plain. The topography of the country is about the same for thousands of miles. The most significant mountain chain on this vast plateau is the Ural Mountains; but they average only about 560 feet in elevation, about as impressive as the Coastal Range of California.

Although on a map Russia is huge, its usable area is much smaller. The really useful part of Russia can be outlined as a giant teardrop tapering off at Lake Baikal. Most of the rest of the country is swamp, tundra and desert. (See map on facing page.)

Geographically, Russia is part of Asia. I hate to disillusion anyone, but Europe is not really a continent. Our ancestors, however, were not content to be a small peninsula of Asia. So they arbitrarily created a continent to separate "Europe" from Asia. The line starts in the Arctic and runs down the unimpressive Ural Mountain range, which is why that range is given undue importance. But the mountains peter out in the south, so they then jumped the line to the Ural River and followed that to the Caspian Sea. All well and good. But then where do we go with this line? You don't want to include Middle-Eastern types in Europe; so they skipped over most of the Caspian Sea and then latched on to the Caucasus Mountains. These would pull the line back to the Black Sea and it was clear sailing from there, over the sea, past Constantinople, and on home. The whole thing is a geographic sham.

The major gap in the geographic defense of Russia is between the southern end of the Ural Mountains and the Caspian Sea. It is through this gap that the fiercest Asiatic hordes poured into Russia. (Asiatic tribes always seem to travel in Hordes.) This was a major invasion route from earliest times right down to the 19th century.

The rivers of Russia have been decisive in her growth. The pattern of settlement from West to East was along the river systems. Hunters and then settlers moved up one river till they came close to another. Then they unloaded their boats, took them apart, and carried everything overland to the next river. The boats were reassembled, reloaded, and taken down that river until they got close to another. In this way they zigzagged their way across the plains of Russia and Siberia all the way to the Pacific. And even after they reached the Pacific (The Sea of Okhotsk) they could not break the habit. Instead of sailing around the Kamchatka Peninsula they sailed up to it, unloaded the boats, took them apart, dragged them across the Peninsula, reassembled them on the other side, reloaded them, and sailed on to Alaska.

All of this was quite exhausting, especially in warm summer

The boundary of Europe and the significant part of Russia

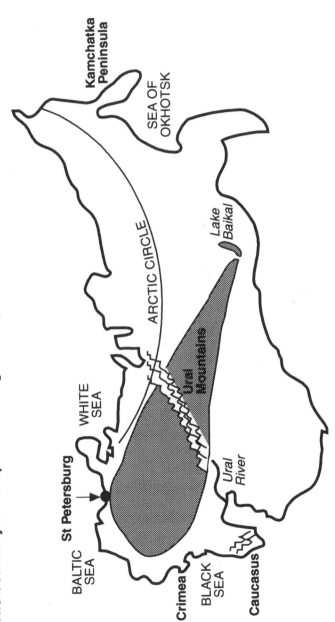

The significant part of Russia

5

months. So the towns of Russia would grow up at these portage points between the rivers. A portage spot was a good place for a tavern, then a hotel, souvenir shop, a drug store for muscle-pain relievers, etc. Moscow is a prime example of a town that governs the portage among seven river systems.

2

KIEVAN RUSSIA

The earliest period of Russian history is the Kievan Period from about 800 to about 1200 A.D. In the 6th century Slavic tribes had pushed eastward from Central Europe to the Dnpr River. They then settled in villages scattered north and south along that river by the 8th century. These towns were attacked from the East by Asiatic invading tribes such as the Pechenegs and the Black Bolgers. Then the Vikings came in from Sweden rowing down the Russian River system. They were called "The Rus", or "Rowers". They gave their name to the country — "The Land of the Rus" or "Russia". They were often welcomed as ones who could help the Slavs defend themselves against other invaders and against one another. During the course of the 9th century these Viking bands took over control of the weak city states of Russia and not without consent. As one Kievan chronicler wrote, they asked the Vikings, "Please rule over us. Bring order". And later, "They brought order. Before, there was no order there". Thus began the Norman period of Russia, the first time the entire state was organized and controlled.

Many contemporary Russian scholars object to this Norman Theory of Russian history. They resent the notion that the Russians had to call in the Swedes to get organized. But I remain unconvinced by their objections because of the lack of contrary evidence.

Two of the earliest rulers were Rurik, over the Principality of Novgorod, and Oleg, his brother ruling the Principality of Kiev, (played in the film by Victor Mature). Their early history was brutal. Oleg's son and successor, Igor, was killed in a battle against the Drevlianians. His widow, Olga, ruled Kiev for the next 17 years (945–962). The Drevlianians sent some envoys in a boat to propose that she marry their prince. Olga had a huge pit dug. She then threw the envoys and their boat into the pit and had them all buried alive. The Drevlianians took this to be a "No" to their marriage proposal.

On another occasion the Drevlianians sent envoys and she invited them into a bathhouse. They got rather excited. But she locked them in and burned the bathhouse. This would discourage future envoys from coming. She then became a Christian and was later made a saint!

The next ruler of note was Vladimir who was also later made a saint. Vladimir ruled Kiev from 978 to 1015. He had 800 wives! He decided to embrace a church and shopped around. He studied the Catholic Church, the Hebrew faith and others and finally decided upon the Eastern Greek Orthodox in 988. The Eastern Byzantine Emperor in Constantinople was delighted and sent his sister up to be wife number 801. There then followed the mass conversion of Russia to Christianity.

From the 9th century until the 13th century Russia was developing much like the rest of Europe and seemed on its way to prosperity from which they could later share in the Renaissance.

But then came the terrible invasions of the 13th century. The Germans marched up the coast to Estonia and threatened Novgorod. But the Prince of Novgorod, Alexander Nevskii, rallied a defense and stopped the Germans in 1242 in a battle on the ice of Lake Peipus on the eastern side of Estonia. This battle is vividly portrayed in the film *Alexander Nevskii* produced in Russia in 1938. This was really an effective propaganda film preparing the Russian people for a future German invasion. It portrays the Germans in a most evil light. Even the slits in their helmets were cut to look evil. The Germans also had an evil-looking monk with a portable organ who played evil music on the bottom four notes of his instrument. The German knights busied themselves burning babies until Nevskii could attack. The whole message was one of "Beware! They are coming again". It is a brilliant piece of cinematography. You would never guess Nevskii was a prince. He was seen romping around Novgorod in the period's equivalent of Levis and T-shirt.

In addition to the German invasion, which established the control of the Teutonic Knights over Estonia and Latvia, the Swedes and the Poles also invaded from the West. This would deprive Russia of a seacoast on the Baltic, and would advance the Polish border to within 100 miles of Moscow.

But of all the dreadful invasions of that unhappy century, by far the worst was that of the Mongols in 1237. The Mongols made a bad impression. They never bathed except in their own urine. So you could always tell when a Mongol entered the room. A Turkish contemporary described them:

> Their stink was more horrible than their color. Their faces were set on their bodies as if they had no neck. Their cheeks resembled soft leather bottles, full of wrinkles and knots. Their noses extended from cheek to cheek. Their nostrils resembled rotten graves, and from them the hair descended as far as their lips.

(And these are the people portrayed in Hollywood by John Wayne and Omar Shariff!) Genghis Khan left us his credo:

> Man's greatest good fortune is to chase and defeat his enemy, seize his total possessions, leave his married women weeping and wailing, ride his gelding, and use the bodies of his women as a nightshirt.

(Words to inspire us all).

They advanced in a tidal wave of horror. The bulk of the Russian population who were not killed fled north from the Dnpr River area to the Volga River region. The area around Kiev, once the rich heartland of Russia, became a wasteland. The city of Kiev was destroyed, the villages and farms were ravaged, there were mass slaughters of the people. Skeletons were scattered all about like the Killing Fields of Cambodia in our own day. The veil of death would be draped over Kiev for centuries.

3

THE RISE OF MUSCOVY

Now Russian history was to diverge from that of Western Europe. Under the yoke of the Mongols trade was blocked, the economy was frozen, the riches of the earlier period were gone. Russia would be held back for centuries just as Europe was emerging from under the shroud of the Dark Ages. But Russia would be economically and culturally frozen for two more centuries. This would have a profound impact on Russian history.

One consequence of this would be periodic efforts to catch up with the West. We shall note this with Peter the Great in the 18th century, Alexander I and Alexander II during the 19th century, Nicholas II at the turn of the century, and all Communist leaders since Lenin. They would all emphasize how far behind Russia was and how they must catch up quickly. This catch-up phobia has been part of the Russian character for 300 years now.

The new post-Mongol center of Russia was to be in the northeast – Moscow. This had been the more backward area of Russia economically, politically and culturally before the fall of Kiev. It was a rather primitive region of small estates and country squires. An Arkansas, in contrast to the Manhattan-like Kiev. But Moscow would have certain critical advantages. First, it had a good central location. It governed the portages reaching seven rivers which would lead to four seas (White, Baltic, Black, Caspian). It would also have the good fortune to have several able rulers, John Wayne types who would build an empire. Moscow also had the advantage of housing the Elder of the Russian Church. He had been in Kiev, moved briefly to Vladimir, then settled in Moscow. This gave the city enormous prestige.

The new center of a resurrected Russia was to be the Principality of Muscovy. Moscow was first mentioned in 12th-century chronicles. The first ruler of the principality to hit the archives was Ivan I (Ivan Moneybags) a clever ruler of the 14th century. He managed to purchase immunity from Mongol interference and then was appointed by the Mongols to be their collector of tribute from other princes. In other words, he was a collaborator! It was also during his reign that the Elder of the Russian Church moved from Vladimir to Moscow.

The next significant ruler of note was Ivan III (The Great) who reigned from 1462 to 1505. He was the first real national ruler of Russia, capturing Novgorod and expanding Muscovy to an area of about 15,000 square miles, about the size of the Netherlands today. He also won independence from the Mongol-Tatar "Golden Horde" and it was he who first fostered the idea of Moscow as "The Third Rome". He had married the niece of the last Byzantine emperor, who had lost his empire to the infidel Turks in 1453. Marrying the Imperial Princess was a big social step up for this rural Russian. It could compare to Buddy Hackett marrying Princess Margaret of England. Sophia was bright, witty and ambitious, like some of our own First Ladies. It is said that behind every great man is a greater woman. That certainly was the case with Ivan the Great. It is said that she was the one to talk him into breaking with the Mongols. She did not use the title "Princess of Moscow". Instead she called herself "Imperial Princess of Byzantium" and must have had all her hankies embroidered with the imperial insignia. Ivan was delighted with her posturing and declared himself ruler of all Russia. He then took upon himself the title of "Tsar", the successor to the Eastern Roman (Byzantine) Emperor. He used the double-headed eagle, the imperial crest of Byzantium as his own. He wore an Imperial Cap and must have had all his shorts embroidered with the Imperial symbol also.

But despite these pretensions, Russia was far behind Europe, a Slavic Dogpatch far to the east of Western civilization. Their only port was Archangel, established in 1533 on the White Sea and only open during the Russian summer (which ran from late July to early August). Ships had to scurry back and forth before the ice froze the sea.

An example of Russia's isolation is the story of a German knight named Poppel who stumbled onto Muscovy in the late 1400s. He was surprised to find a country there and reported the fact to the German Emperor, Frederick III. Frederick was also surprised to hear there was a country east of Poland which was not under the Mongols. In proper emperor fashion, Frederick offered Ivan the title of "King" and also offered him the hand of a Habsburg niece in marriage (there were plenty of nieces to go around). Ivan replied politely with thanks but said he was already married. And besides, why should he settle for the title of "King" when he was already an Emperor and his imperial authority came directly from God! (I wish I could have seen Frederick's face when he got that letter.)

While Russia was building its meager power on the international scene, there was rising internal tension between the increasing power of the Tsar and the entrenched nobility who did not want to lose power to a central authority. It was a case of an irresistible force meeting an immovable object. Such conflicts were common in Europe during the early modern period as central royal authority began to encroach upon the feudal rights of nobles. In Russia this tension would lead to "The Time of Troubles" at the end of the 1500s.

The Tsars were building their power base on a new class of "Service Nobility" who served the state for life (usually in the military) in exchange for landed estates. There was no significant middle class in Russia, so the Service Nobility was a kind of substitute. But the powerful old Boyar class felt threatened.

The peasants of Russia had been free tenant farmers around 1500, but would find themselves bound to the land as serfs by 1600 (just as serfs were wrenching themselves to freedom in Western Europe). Many peasants fled to the frontiers, especially in the south, and became "Cossacks", a kind of cowboy. The term is from the Turkish meaning "Freeman" or "Rebel". The government tolerated this since they needed people to defend the frontiers. So the government would give them land and they were to turn a share of the crop over to the local fort.

The Tsar Ivan the Terrible died in 1584. His older son, Feodor, was an imbecile. The Polish Ambassador wrote, "Of mind hath he but little". Nevertheless, they made him Tsar (imbecility has not been an impediment to the rise of many national leaders in modern history). Ivan had a younger son, Dmitry, but he died as the result of an accident when he was two or three years old. So Feodor the Imbecile was made Tsar and ruled from 1584 to 1598. (Incidentally, he was not called that. You would not greet him by saying "Good Morning Your Imbecility".) The Boyars did not mind Feodor's reign. They appointed a committee of regency to rule while Feodor lay on the floor licking a table leg or something. The Regency Committee included a Tatar Boyar, Boris Godunov. Gradually the other regents disappeared and Boris Godunov was left in charge. (I suspect foul play.) Feodor the Imbecile died in 1598 and Boris got the lesser nobles to elect him Tsar. The old-time Boyer nobles were furious. They looked upon Boris as a Mongol upstart.

This succession contest came at a time when Russia was facing a quadruple crisis:

- A famine, with accompanying economic misery
- Peasant unrest
- Foreign intervention
- The appearance of a man claiming to be Ivan's younger son Dmitry! We will call him "False Dmitry Number One".

To dispel the claims of False Dmitry Number One, Boris Godunov appointed a commission to find out if the real Dmitry was really dead. The investigation concluded that the real Dmitry had cut himself with a knife and died in an epileptic fit. But False Dmitry really believed he was Ivan's son. He had evidently been groomed for this all his life by Polish conspirators. They had hoped to control all Russia, and to convert Russia to Catholicism with Dmitry on the throne.

False Dmitry entered Russia in 1604 with some Polish troops. He was joined by thousands of Cossacks and by Boyars who hated Boris Godunov. The next year, 1605, Boris died. His son was killed and his wife and sister were sent off to a convent as reluctant nuns. The people of Moscow wanted Dmitry. He entered the city with great fanfare and was made Tsar! An imposter!

To authenticate him the authorities called in Ivan the Great's widow. "Is this your son?" they asked. She quickly agreed, "Yes that's my boy!" Why did she do this? Well, as the mother of the Tsar she would have all kinds of privileges and influence, (charge account at Niemen Marcus at least). If she denied him, and someone else was made Tsar, she might end up as another reluctant nun in some convent. So she embraced him.

But Dmitry soon shocked Moscow and lost support. He ignored convention. He shaved his beard, so he did not look like the Lord. He wore Western clothing. He kept his Polish retinue. He worked hard and ate fast unlike other Tsars. He did not go to church. (As Tsar he should have gone two or three times a day.) So people thought him a very strange Tsar. And the Poles were disappointed because they could not control him. The Boyars were also disappointed because they could not control him. And so a conspiracy was hatched. A group of Boyars killed him and claimed he was not the true Tsar. How could this be? They called in Ivan's widow again. "Was that your boy?" they asked. She replied, "Well, no. At first I thought it was; but his eyes just did not have that twinkle of my Dmitry". Why did she reverse herself? Again to save her life and stay out of the convent. Dmitry's body was cut up into pieces, the pieces were burned, the ashes packed in a cannon, and he was shot back toward Poland from whence he had come (though rumors persisted that he had escaped).

The Boyars now chose one of their own, a Vasilii Shuiskii as Tsar. His first act was to dispel the rumor that Dmitry had escaped. To do this he had the original Dmitry canonized! This dead three-year-old was made a saint! And behold! Miracles were associated with his body. This proved he was a saint and the real Dmitry.

But rumors persisted that Dmitry was alive, that somehow he had escaped from the cannon and patched himself up with an enormous quantity of bandaids. There arose a peasant rebel named Bolotnikov, who said he was acting for Dmitry who was hiding. Bolotnikov had a simple social-political program. He advocated freeing all the peasants, giving them the land, and exterminating the Boyars. This program did not sit well with the

Boyers; so they defeated his forces and Bolotnikov disappeared. (I suspect foul play.)

Then a new threat arose in 1607. A man came out of Poland claiming to be Dmitry! That he had somehow escaped from the cannon. This would be False Dmitry Number Two. This one was a complete adventurer and an ex-convict. But people were so fed up with Vasilii that Dmitry immediately got a large following (the Ross Perot syndrome). Civil war ensued. The Poles and Swedes happily jumped into the fray. The Poles captured Smolensk and planned to rule all Russia. But then they were defeated. Vasilii was thrown out and sent to a monastery as a reluctant monk. False Dmitry Number Two advanced to the gates of Moscow. But then he was captured and killed. For three years, 1610–1613, Russia had no Tsar.

4

RISE OF THE ROMANOVS

Russia was confused without a Tsar. So in 1613 the nobles gathered together and looked around for a weak candidate to be Tsar. They did not want a strong leader to challenge their powers. They wanted a wimp. They chose Michael Romanov, a weak, sickly youngster of 17. He was for them an ideal choice. They did not realize that although he was weak, he would have some great descendants.

Russia drifted through the 17th century without great leadership. Serfdom was formalized as a system binding the peasants to the land. No one was free except the Cossacks. Russia did, however, complete her expansion to the Pacific through waves of hunters, traders and settlers. Siberia, north of troublesome Asian hordes, was colonized by Russians roughly between 1550 and 1650.

The next major move in Russian history was to come about because of another powerful personality, Peter the Great (1689–1725). The Tsar Feodor had died in 1682. Peter was only ten years old. He had a feeble-minded older half-brother, Ivan, and a half-sister, Sophia. The Boyars chose Peter to be Tsar. This meant that his mother would dominate Russia as regent. But Sophia refused to accept this. She hatched a plot. There was rioting in the Kremlin. As a result, Peter and Ivan were made co-Tsars with half-sister Sophia as regent. Peter was then sent off to the country with his Mom who simply wanted to sulk. His Mom ignored Peter, so he grew up very uncouth. He played with kids in the village and finally gathered about 100 boys who wanted to

Russia's Neighbours at the Time of Peter the Great

play war. Peter asked his Mom if they could have uniforms and arms. His Mom said "Yes, don't bother me, I'm sulking". In 1689 this group of boys had become a finely tuned military force. Peter was now 17. He marched into Moscow, seized power and sent his half-sister Sophia off to a convent as another reluctant nun. Peter would now rule Russia alone.

He was an imposing figure of a man. He was nearly seven feet tall. He was very strong and could bend pokers if anyone asked. He was wild, noisy, a heavy drinker, quick tempered, and rather cruel. Once he had some traitors hanged and had the body of Sophia's uncle dug up and put under the scaffold so the blood would drip on it. A strange man.

Peter decided to visit Western Europe incognito 1697–1698. His disguise was a poor one. He had a large entourage. Everyone recognized him; but they went along with the game. He first visited Riga, (then under Sweden). He got mad at the Swedes because they would not let him see their fortifications. (This poor Swedish public relations failure was to have dire consequences later.) He then went to Königsberg where the Prussians treated him very well. They taught him how to shoot cannon, etc. He then went on to Hanover in northern Germany where he was invited to a ball given by the Electress herself. He was a social failure at the ball. For the first hour or so he sat in a corner covering his face with his hands. (I can see everyone asking the Electress, "Who is the creep in the corner?".) After a while he softened up and joined the party. He was amazed at dancing, and the painted faces of the ladies. He was confused by whalebones in ladies' corsets and thought the ladies of Germany had extra bones in their bodies. From this social disaster he went on to Holland where he was fascinated by the construction of ships. He then went on to England, sat in the Strangers' Gallery and was disgusted with Parliamentarianism. Then on to Venice and back home to Russia.

During his journey Peter tried to interest other countries in carving up the Turkish Empire; but he could find no one interested in a slice of Turkey. Several did say, however, that if he ever went after Sweden to give them a call. They might be interested in joining him. This idea was to fester in his mind. The other conclusion Peter reached after a year of travel in the West was the realization of how backward Russia was. He would become obsessed with the idea of catching up with the West.

To establish contact with the West, Peter wanted a warm-water port. Those on the Black Sea seemed more remote and he might not have allies. So he attacked Sweden in 1700. It seemed a good time to attack Sweden because the new King there, Charles XII, was a strange kid of 15. He liked to break windows. He liked to throw furniture out of the windows without opening them. He enjoyed beheading sheep (which should alarm any mother). He liked to shoot people. Every day it was arranged for him to have a pistol (loaded with blanks), then have a servant walk across the courtyard. After the shot the servant would collapse clutching his chest, and he would be carried off. Charles also enjoyed kicking trays out of the hands of servants, then running giggling down the corridor. The point is, Sweden had a leadership problem.

As soon as the war began, Denmark, Poland and Brandenburg joined Russia to carve up the Swedish Empire. But Charles, to everyone's surprise, unhampered by formal military training, turned out to be a great general! He was bold and daring. He would move armies farther and faster than you were supposed to. And so the war, anticipated as brief, was to last over 20 years until 1721.

Early in the war, in 1703, the Russians captured a Swedish fort in a marshy area at the mouth of the Neva River. Shortly afterward a Dutch ship sailed into the harbor and was surprised by a wild Russian welcome party. Here Peter would build his 'Window on the West', his warm water port. He would also construct his new modern Western capital city. The construction of St. Petersburg is a gruesome story. Some 40,000 serfs died from disease, their bodies pushed under with the wooden pilings to shore up the new city. In the end they did build a beautiful city, although today after some 70 years of Communist neglect it looks rather shabby.

The construction of St. Petersburg began what I would call "The Russian Tale of Two Cities: Moscow and St. Petersburg". Moscow represents traditional, isolated, suspicious Russia. It is the semi-Oriental interior, a provincial capital withdrawn from the Western world. St. Petersburg, on the other hand, represents the sophisticated, modern Russia – a Western, 18th century city

19

reaching out to the West and to modern times.

The Swedes were drawn deep into Russia and were beaten at Poltava in the Ukraine in 1709. Charles later died and the Swedes finally made peace in 1721 yielding to Russia the Baltic Coast from Viborg, near present-day Finland, to Riga, in present-day Latvia. Peter had established Russia as a major European power.

Peter's internal reforms were devoted to the Europeanization of Russia. He wanted to move away from the Oriental Boris Godunov image, to a modern 18th-century one. He ordered Russian nobles to cut off their beards and to trim their greatcoats, which touched the ground. There were practical and religious objections to this. The beards and greatcoats helped during Russia's cold winters. And beards were important because God meant men to have them. They made one resemble the Lord. Peasants were exempt from these regulations. They seemed beyond help. But the nobles were supposed to obey. Peter personally cut off the beards and coats of many at court. Many nobles resisted and continued to wear beards secretly under their collars (which must have looked funny), or kept them in their pockets for Judgment Day.

Peter also decreed that all nobles must be able to read. And he declared that no noble could get married until he had passed a reading test. This caused a literacy crisis. Tutors were rushed all over Russia to give cram courses in reading. I can just see Natasha writing her fiancé, "For God's sake, Ivan, hurry up. The invitations are out and I am in my third month!" Meanwhile poor Ivan is struggling with "See Spot! See Spot run!".

In addition, while Peter did not take away any noble privileges, he decreed that they must all serve the state in the army or some substitute service, for life.

5

THE 18TH CENTURY

The 18th century was schizophrenic. We are all aware of the graceful surface world of the Baroque – the elegant music, art, architecture and way of life of the nobility. But there was also an ugly sub-surface world of human suffering welling up into an explosive revolutionary spirit. On the one hand you have an elegant ball at the Versailles Palace, on the other hand a group of ragged revolutionaries in downtown Paris huddled around a candle and plotting revolution. I sometimes compare this dual image of that century with a beautiful wedding cake crawling with maggots.

In Russia the serfs were being degraded more and more almost to the point of slavery. The nobles were released from their obligation to serve the state and became a group of frivolous parasites taking much from society and giving nothing. The Tsars would rule during that century increasingly by capricious whim rather than by sober reflection of national interests.

The capricious nature of Russian dynastic politics can be seen in the confused succession after Peter the Great. The crown was tossed about like a football. You need to study the chart on page 22 to keep abreast of what was happening. (The dates show the period of each reign.)

Peter the Great (A) was disappointed in his son Alexis. He wanted his grandson to succeed instead. His son was put on trial for conspiracy and died during the trial, probably from torture. Then Peter died, unexpectedly, in 1725. The nobles were afraid to give the crown to Peter's grandson since they were implicated in

SUCCESSION TO THE RUSSIAN THRONE IN THE 18TH CENTURY

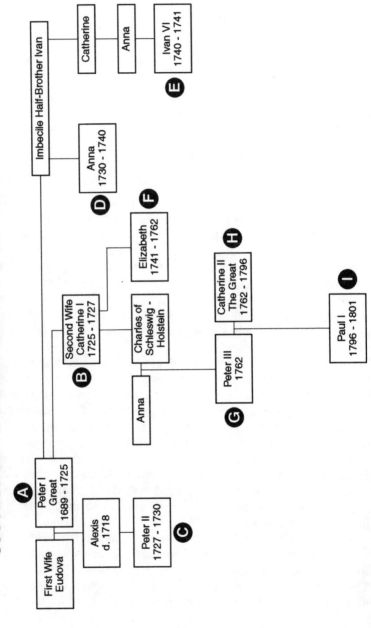

22

the death of his father and he might seek revenge. So they chose Peter's second wife Catherine I (B) to be Tsarina.

This was not Catherine the Great. We might call her "Catherine the Pretty Good". She was a wine merchant's daughter with whom Peter lived in sin while his first wife was alive. As soon as they met their eyelids fluttered, their bosoms heaved, it was love at first sight. Peter sent his wife off to a convent as another reluctant nun and kept Catherine as his mistress until his wife died, probably from an overdose of abstinence. As soon as she was gone, Peter married Catherine.

Catherine was very popular with the Guards, for good reason, but she died after only two years. At this point Peter the Great's grandson (C) was chosen, but he only ruled for three years, then he died.

They then chose Peter the Great's niece, Anna (D), daughter of his imbecile half-brother Ivan. She ruled from 1730 to 1740 with the aid of her lover, Biron the Horse Tender. Under Anna's reign the serfs of Russia declined in status to their nadir. They could now be flogged, jailed, or sold with or without the land. The government only intervened in extreme cases. There was one sadistic noblewoman at this time who had tortured 140 serfs to death. Her punishment was to watch a serf being flogged (which she probably enjoyed) then she was sent off to a convent as a problem nun. All of this had profound social importance for the future history of Russia.

Anna had chosen her baby nephew Ivan to succeed as Ivan VI 1740–1741 (E) with her lover Biron the Horse Tender, as regent. But the guards hated Biron and soon chose the daughter of Peter the Great, Elizabeth (F), to rule. Elizabeth, daughter of Peter and his wine merchant's-daughter mistress was illegitimate until Peter married her mother. She ruled from 1741 to 1762 and was played in the film by Bette Davis. She was very pretty and was also popular with the Guards, also for good reason. She agreed to be Empress because the alternative, a convent, was unthinkable both for her and the convent. When she assumed power she kissed the baby Tsar Ivan (E) and had him imprisoned.

Elizabeth was a very popular monarch because she was both very religious and very immoral. She appealed to saints and sinners alike, both the upper and lower classes. She went to war against Prussia in 1756 because Frederick the Great had been writing nasty things about her, all of which were true, but were intercepted by her spies. When she died in 1762 they could not make the baby Ivan Tsar again because he was hopelessly insane after 20 years of solitary confinement. So they chose her nephew, Peter III (G), who would only rule six months.

Peter III was drunk from the age of ten. And he was strange. As an adult he liked to play with toy soldiers, which most men stop doing by their 30s. Once a rat damaged one of his soldiers. He had the rat arrested and formally tried by a court martial of the highest generals of the land. The court martial found the rat guilty and he was ceremoniously hanged. So we must conclude Peter was strange.

Peter was married to a minor German Princess, Catherine (H) from Pomerania. He hated his wife and constantly humiliated her. She was afraid for her life. Incidentally, Peter III is the last Tsar called Peter. You might say the Romanovs Petered out at this point, especially since Catherine said the father of her son was one of the guards.

Although Peter hated Catherine, she was very popular with the Guards. And for good reason. She had 21 known lovers. But she was terrified that Peter might send her off to a nunnery, which would be intolerable both for her and for the other nuns. So she joined in a conspiracy to seize power and in the process Peter was killed.

Catherine (played in the show *Catherine WAS Great* by Mae West) was now Empress! During her reign, court life became quite shocking and historians never cease to write about it so we can all be shocked. There were wild parties and even exaggerated accounts of orgies. She arranged for one of her lovers to be elected King of Poland. But he would not follow her orders, so Poland was slated to be partitioned. The Emperor Josef of Austria once visited her and she seduced him, winning an Austrian alliance for Russia. She was always willing to give her all for Russia. Catherine's reign also witnessed great expansion, not only of Catherine but also of Russia. She arranged the annexation of two-thirds of Poland as well as the northern coast of the Black Sea.

And she went on to scheme about further expansion to the Turkish Straits. She once spoke of a future Russian empire with six capitals: St. Petersburg, Moscow, Astrakan, Constantinople, Vienna and Berlin! This did not sit well in Constantinople, Vienna and Berlin.

Catherine died in 1796 probably from natural causes, though court scandal-mongers spread vicious gossip that she died because of a romantic entanglement with a horse during which she was crushed to death. One hears this story from time to time from local guides anxious to augment their tips.

It might be mentioned that Catherine's coming to the throne was a blessing for California and the United States. The Russian-American Company was having a difficult time maintaining a foothold in North America. They had extended their influence as far south as Fort Ross in Sonoma County, California. But they needed a food base. They once tried to infiltrate Hawaii, but backed the wrong side in a civil war there and lost out. They asked for help from the Tsarina. But Catherine belonged to the Enlightenment book-of-the-month club and had read Adam Smith who argued that nature should govern economics without government aid. So Catherine rejected the appeal of the Russian-American Company.

There was one other possibility for Russian-America, and that was an alliance with Spanish California. In the early 19th century the Russian-American Company got a new governor. A handsome, dashing officer, Count Rezanov. He sailed into San Francisco Bay in 1806 seeking food from the Spaniards who were worried about the Yankee drive westward. American forces had pushed as far west as Dodge City under the leadership of John Wayne and were anxious to expand to the Pacific ("Manifest Destiny"*). The Spaniards thought an alliance with Russian-America might forever block the Yankees at Salt Lake. So when Rezanov came to California he was given a warm reception.

Even warmer was the reception given Rezanov by Donna Concepción, daughter of the Spanish governor. When she and

---

* The deepseated American conviction that the USA was destined to expand all the way to the Pacific coast.

Rezanov saw one another their eyelids fluttered, their bosoms heaved, it was love at first sight. They wanted to get married, but because of religious differences she had to contact the Pope and Rezanov had to check with the Tsar. He sailed out of San Francisco harbor to report to the Tsar. Donna Concepción waved goodbye at the dock. She waited, she waited and she waited. Rezanov never came back! It was later learned that he had died on his trip across Siberia. Donna Concepción could wed no other, because she and Rezanov had already wed with their eyes (This is romantic love, quite different from today's hectic rush to a motel.) So she joined a convent and spent the rest of her life in Mission Dolores in San Francisco. She became a legend in her old age as San Franciscans, in the 1870s, talked about this legendary nun in Mission Dolores. She died and was buried there in the Mission garden. Thus ends one of the great romances of California history. Had Rezanov succeeded, the Russians and the Spanish might have joined hands through this marriage and held the Americans back at the Rocky Mountain line!

Catherine was succeeded by her son Paul (I), who was so strange, her husband Peter must have been the father. Paul had a brief and eccentric reign from 1796–1801. He hated his mother and those who supported her. He hated the French Revolution and forbade the wearing of any three colors for fear of the tricolor. He decreed that when his carriage passed ladies were to get out of their carriages and curtsy in the muddy streets of St. Petersburg. He once ordered a sloppy regiment to march to Siberia, and they did! He then ordered some 30,000 Cossacks on the Don River to mount their horses and ride to India! This was too much. A conspiracy was hatched and he was killed.

6

THE 19TH CENTURY

Paul was succeeded by his son, Alexander I (1801–1825) who would be the Tsar to face Napoleon. Alexander was a moody ruler who had an ever-changing personality. He lived during the week with his father in a very austere, dour setting. Then he would go off for weekends with his Grandmama Catherine for fun and games. Every weekend was whoopie time. So his moods could change suddenly and radically.

Napoleon, played in the film by Marlon Brando, invaded Russia in 1812 with his *Grand Armée* of 600,000. For defense the Russians relied on space, mud and winter weather. The Russians kept retreating, forcing the French to stretch their supply lines. Napoleon was counting on a quick battle to destroy the Russian Army and make peace. But the Russians responded mainly with guerilla warfare and a scorched-earth policy. The Russians eventually fought a couple of battles, which weakened the French, but did not defeat them. There is an appropriate statue marking one of these battles in Smolensk showing the French Eagle with his wings clipped.

Another factor in the French defeat was a young girl from Martinique, Aimee Dubuque de Rivery, a cousin of Josephine, Napoleon's wife. Aimee and Josephine were Creole girls who grew up together on the Caribbean island. When Josephine came of age she was sent to France to complete her education and find a suitable husband. She married Eugene Beauharnais, a French aristocrat. Later Josephine (played in the film by Merle Oberon) married Napoleon and became Empress of France. Aimee had gone to

27

France to attend a convent school. Returning to Martinique in 1784, aged 21, her ship was captured by pirates under the command of the Bey of Algiers. At the time she was captured, the Bey was trying to think of things to send as his annual tribute to the Turkish Sultan in Istanbul. Along with the cloth, leather goods, jewelry, etc. he sent Aimee for the Sultan's harem. Aimee quickly adjusted well to her new position and ended up as the Sultan's favorite and mother of the heir to the throne. This meant she was in effect "Empress" of the Ottoman Empire! One biographer refers to her as "The Sultana". So two little girls from Martinique ended up doing very well as Empresses!

Aimee's life in the harem was kept secret. She could not have contact with her family because she was a fallen woman. But she did have influence at court and this was significant. Her son became Mahmoud II in 1808. In 1810 Napoleon dumped Josephine and married Maria Luisa Habsburg. This not only gave him social prestige but it practically guaranteed him an heir which he was desperately anxious to have. (Habsburgs were noted for having 10 to 20 children). Aimee was furious about what he had done to her cousin and girlhood friend. In 1812, when Napoleon was getting ready to invade Russia, he noted that Turkey was at war with Russia. So he urged the Sultan to keep up the pressure from the south. But when Aimee heard that she told her son, "Don't you dare help that dreadful man!" The Sultan replied, "Yes mother", and made peace with Russia. This released the pressure from the south so the Russians could concentrate on defeating Napoleon. We cannot say this was decisive in Napoleon's defeat. But certainly some credit is due to the girlhood friendship in the Caribbean which affected this major turn in the history of Europe.

Napoleon advanced as far as Moscow and waited for the Russians to surrender. But they did not. What could he now do? He could order his army to turn left and march 800 miles to St. Petersburg. But what good would that do? The Russian government could simply move its file cabinet to Tomsk and Napoleon would have to march several hundred more miles. This is the problem trying to defeat Russia. There is no central nerve point which, if taken, would cripple the enemy. If an invader takes Paris, France is doomed. But Russia is like a huge dinosaur, with a brain the size

28

of a walnut. You can probe all over but have a devil of a time trying to find it.

Napoleon waited in Moscow for a Russian peace offer. None came. It started to get cold. He was urged to withdraw, which he finally decided to do late in October. His retreat during November became a route in the fierce cold. Russian troops would strike suddenly at the French flanks and rear. Napoleon's forces dwindled in size. By the time they got back to the Prussian border from whence they had invaded Russia, only about 60,000 men, or 10 per cent, was left of the proud *Grand Armée* which had entered the country in June.

This disaster encouraged the rising of Europe against Napoleon and his final defeat in 1815. In the peace settlement Russia managed to keep Finland, which they had earlier seized from Sweden, as well as most of Poland. Russian troops had marched all the way across Europe to Paris. Russia was now a major power.

The post-Napoleonic period started with a fresh political breeze in Russia. Russian officers, leading their armies across Europe, came into contact with new Western ideas about constitutions, freedom, liberalism, etc. It affected them to the point that upon the death of Alexander I in 1825 they pushed for a constitution in a modest revolt. They were called "The Decembrists" since that is when the uprising took place. They wanted Constantine as Tsar instead of the legitimate heir, his brother Nicholas. It was pathetic to hear innocent supportive peasants ignorant of the issues crying "Constantine and Constitutia!" thinking Constitutia was his wife!

The revolt was soon suppressed and Russia slid back into archaic despotism under Tsar Nicholas I. But it reminds us of a similar problem during World War II. For over 20 years Soviet citizens had been told by their Communist government how much the masses of Europe had been suffering under the yolk of monopoly-capitalism. But as their troops advanced toward the Elbe River they saw how much better off the workers of the West were than their cohorts living in the "Socialist Paradise". So all these troops had to be run through intellectual de-lousing stations called "Anti-Facist Schools" or "Anitfa Schools". There they were told that although things looked good in the West (running water, leather shoes, etc.) it was really a sick society on the brink of collapse. The Soviets maintained these schools after the war to process their soldiers returning from occupation duty in the "decadent West".

The next major event of Russian history after Napoleon was the Crimean War (1853–1856). It was a sordid war that no one wanted and no one knew how to fight. But it seemed impossible to prevent. The problem began with disputes over certain holy sites in the Holy Land. Some sacred shrines, like the Church of the Holy Sepulchre were run jointly by several churches, the predominant being the Greek Orthodox and the Roman Catholic. Squabbles arose such as whose turn it was to use the altar, or sweep up, and fights broke out with clergy throwing things at one another. The Greek Orthodox looked to the Tsar as their protector and the Roman Catholics looked to Louis Napoleon of France. The Tsar then declared himself the Protector of all Christians throughout the Ottoman Empire – a claim that could menace the sovereignty of Turkey.

The Sultan was worried that if he did nothing, the powers might consider a partition of his empire. So he deliberately provoked a crisis. He declared war on Russia. Then he sailed his decrepit old fleet up to the Russian one and paraded it up and down. So the Russians sank it. This aroused a howl of protest in the West against the barbaric, aggressive Russians! It was called "The Massacre of Sinope". Britain went to war against Russia, so France did also.

British and French forces landed in the Balkans and started to march north toward the Danube. Austria was alarmed. They did not want the Russians entering the Balkans, so they declared their neutrality then occupied Romania and told everyone to stay away. The Austrians had removed the battlefield!

The allies were confused, then decided they had to transfer their armies to the nearest Russian territory, the Crimea. There then followed a tragic winter, the only point of light being the lamp of Florence Nightingale. Both sides handled the war poorly. Their armies had rusted since Waterloo. But the Russians were the most poorly led. Russia lost this war on their home ground because they had poor leadership, and their armies were poorly supplied.

Russia actually lost more men on their way to the war than in the war itself.

This had a profound effect upon the Russian government, now led by Tsar Alexander II (The "Tsar Liberator") who came to the throne in 1855. Russian leaders noted that the average Russian soldier did not have his heart in the war and did not fight well. So they concluded that Russia would have to reform if it were to survive. They would have to make the leap from the 17th century to the 19th, to win the allegiance of their people, to give the people a stake in the state so they would be willing to defend it. Otherwise Russia might go under.

This meant a drastic reform of Russian society more profound than the Tsar dreamed of in 1861 when he took his first step on the road to reform by liberating the serfs (over half-a-century behind Western Europe, but two years ahead of the American liberation of slaves). Although serfs were freed, they were not given their land. They would have to buy it over a 49-year period! So, in effect, the government said, "You are free. Here is your 49-year mortgage to pay for this land you have farmed for generations". To manage this payment the peasants were to live in communes (*mirs*) as they had for centuries. Village elders would arrange redistribution of the land of the commune every ten years based on the number of adult working men in each family. So no family really owned its land.

This was not the kind of liberation the serfs had anticipated. They were to pay off the nobility for about half the land of Russia (and they probably were not given the better half) until 1910. This would prove a grave disappointment, which would start to drive the peasants of Russia toward radicalism, unlike peasants in the rest of Europe who remained staunch conservatives.

Once the serfs were freed, the government realized a host of other reforms were needed. Until 1861 the serfs were under the management of local nobles who were the local administrators, draft boards, judges, etc. Now they no longer had this responsibility. So the government had to proceed with further reforms establishing a system of local administration and justice. They also reduced the compulsory military term. Before the Liberation, if you were drafted, you had to serve a 25-year hitch! One can imagine the types who would be selected by local leaders for the army. If they had to send an annual recruit, it would probably be the town drunk or village idiot rather than a hard-working farmer-type. Now the term was only six years. So you could look forward to coming home one day and picking up the pieces of civilian life.

It was also realized that Russians needed better education if they were to have the administrators, judges, engineers, teachers, etc. necessary for a modern state. But the government went back and forth on education for half-a-century. They encouraged universities; but these soon became hotbeds for radicalism and revolution. How do you educate people to think creatively in engineering, but not in politics?

It was an impossible situation. First they would loosen up on universities to get graduates. The students would get radical. Then they would clamp down. So they were not getting the graduates they needed. They would loosen up again. They tried tampering with the curriculum, requiring a lot of mathematics, classical language study and chemistry, etc. But this did not work. A chemistry professor might say, "This is Chemistry 101. But before you learn chemistry you must know philosophy". Then he would launch into a lecture on the evils of the present system until he was arrested and Chemistry 101 was closed. But they needed it for graduation. So he would be released. Those studying classical languages read the ancient philosophers who argued for virtue and freedom. And so it went. The authorities could never figure out how to split the mind to be creative in certain realms but not in others.

Russia had so far to go! And so little time. Tsar Alexander tried to ride the crest of reform but like so many reformers, he simply excited the masses for more change more quickly and was assassinated by radicals in 1881.

Russia was on the slippery slope to radicalism. The peasants were willing to embrace Marxism because they did not own their own land. In 1903 Lenin broke off from the mainstream of Russian socialism by forming his own group, the Bolsheviks. The socialist movement in Europe was suffering during the second half of the 19th century because, contrary to Marx's predictions, things were getting better for workers instead of worse. Those in

32

power were granting real reforms including voting rights and social welfare benefits to the workers. How can this be explained away in Marxian terms?

Lenin proclaimed to his little group that Marx was never wrong. Then he added that Marx was wrong because he had overlooked another stage of history, the Imperialist Stage. He argued that the capitalists had driven the workers of Europe to a near-revolutionary state. To avoid revolution, they had granted some scraps to appease them, and had transferred the exploitation of the European masses to the masses overseas in colonies. The monopoly capitalists could wrench such enormous profits from overseas imperialism, they could afford a few things for the workers back home. So, although things looked good in Europe, this was really the dying stage of capitalism according to Lenin.

Lenin also argued for a small disciplined Communist Party. He felt that most socialists of Europe had become moderates, were accepting reforms from the upper classes, were running for elections, etc. Lenin denounced them as betrayers of the working classes. The party must be a small one, not one with a broad democratic base (I think as a bourgeois he really had contempt for the masses as so many champions of the masses do). The revolution would have to be forceful and violent. In saying this he was really admitting that history had to be pushed along. The revolution was not to be inevitable as Marx had predicted. So Leninism, in many ways, is testimony to the failure of Marxism.

7

RUSSIA ON THE EVE OF REVOLUTION

By the turn of the century it looked as though Russia might finally be catching up with the West. There were great economic strides starting in the 1890s. The Industrial Revolution was catching on there at last. The Communists would later claim that Russia owed her industrialization to the planned efforts of their regime after 1917. But if you extended the economic growth curve starting in the 1890s, the Communist curve would only surpass it in about 1940. This is assuming no wars, famines or other catastrophies, avoidable or otherwise, which plagued Communist Russia. The point is, things were improving in the economy as our century began and one cannot help but wonder what might have happened had there been no World War I and no Communist Revolution. Where would the Russian economy be today?

There was increased political suppression of minority groups, the Finns, Jews, etc. The Jews were the only middle class in Tsarist Russia. They filled a critical need in commerce that no others could fill. Yet they were resented by the nobles and peasants (who needed them). As Russians embraced nationalism, the Jews in particular were to suffer as seen in *Fiddler on the Roof*.

Despite growth in industrial production, the system of government was increasingly unable to cope with a rising economy. Russian society was outgrowing its political system.

The brief war with Japan, 1904–5, showed how backward Russia was. The Japanese had struck in 1904 by sinking the Russian Pacific Fleet. So the Russians sent their European fleet out and the Japanese sank that one too. They also clobbered

Russian forces on land, overrunning Korea and much of Manchuria. This was a national humiliation! An unknown Asian upstart had defeated the Russian Empire!

Russian soldiers suffered from low morale. They were not anxious to fight. The peasant economy was collapsing. There were mutinies in the countryside. Peasants were flocking into the cities to join the ranks of the unemployed.

At this point, by 1905, there was a rising tide of public impatience with the aging Tsarist system. On January 22, 1905, a protest demonstration marched on the Imperial Palace with demands for reform. Shots were fired and some 70 demonstrators were killed. The Russian people spontaneously embraced a General Strike. It was a remarkable demonstration of a people who were fed up. Economic life came to a halt. In desperation the Tsar promised a constitution (a century behind western powers). And elections were soon held for their first legislature, the Duma. But the franchise was so severely restricted, the elected group that emerged was a very reactionary one. It looked like Russia was going nowhere to get out of the mess created by a rising industrial society and an archaic political system.

One valiant eleventh-hour attempt was made to change things. Just before World War I the Stolypin reform program was begun. Count Stolypin had noted that the peasants of Russia, herded into communes, were being radicalized. This was so different from France in the 1790s when the peasants owned the land and were staunch defenders of monarchy and conservatism. Count Stolypin wanted to convert the peasantry of Russia to a conservative force as a base for the monarchy. He wanted the peasants to own their land, to do away with the commune system. If he had more time he might have succeeded. But radicals were afraid of his reforms, which they saw making capitalists out of the peasants. So radicals assassinated Stolypin in 1911. This, in my judgment, meant doom for the monarchy.

With this assassination, Tsarist Russia began her last agonizing mile to catastrophe. The war would come too soon. The Tsarist system would be strained to the breaking point. Under the pressures of war, the system would collapse.

World War I like most wars was a product of human misjudgment. There had been international crises before and, in all of these, someone would back down. The Russian government had retreated before German bluster in 1908 over a Balkan problem because Russia was too weak to face a war. Wracked with revolution, and still smarting from the defeat by the Japanese in 1905, Russia was unable to stand by her fellow Slavs in the Bosnia crisis of 1908.

Then came the crisis of 1914. And this time, no one backed down. Initially, when the Austrian Archduke was shot, no one thought this would lead to a big war. Surely the diplomats would get together as they had time and again during the previous century to work out a peaceful settlement. But it was not to be. Russia felt she could not turn her back on the South Slavs again as she had in 1908, and she was confident of French support to scare the Austrians off. The Austrians, however, were counting on German support to scare the Russians off. But no one was scared off. The Tsar felt he had to stand by the Serbs and not let them be conquered by the Austrians.

The Tsar was in an awkward position. He had no support from the Left. His only support came from the Right and they were heavily Pan-Slavic. They wanted to stand by the Serbs, their fellow Slavic Orthodox Christians. If Nicholas had turned his back on them he would have no support except that of his wife. So everyone stood firm and war became inevitable.

Diplomacy is only as effective as the threat of force behind it. So a power must be prepared to use force to attain a national objective if needed. Although the war was on, everyone was counting on a quick victory. Russia went to war woefully unprepared. There was on average only one gun for every ten men on the front. One would shoot till he fell, then the next one would pick up the rifle and so on. And they might be allotted only two bullets a day against hordes of Teutons! This caused morale to slump.

Initially the Russians advanced into East Prussia, lured into the swamps there by the German Commanders Hindenburg and Ludendorff. The Germans then surrounded the Russians and at the Battle of Tannenburg (August 26–September 15, 1914), they completely annihilated the Russian Army. The Russians lost some

300,000 men. When the Commander, General Samsonov, saw what had happened, he did the only sensible thing. He shot himself. From this point on, the Russians were to retreat. A line of trenches was dug from the Baltic ultimately to the Black Sea, a line that was constantly being pushed back deeper into Russia.

Not only did military morale slump, but morale on the home front also suffered. There were food shortages because the transport system was inadequate. They could not get food from areas of production to areas of consumption. And local distribution failed. So there would be hunger in cities while food rotted in the countryside (like today).

Russia was desperate for supplies. They could not get supplies through the Baltic or Black Sea. There was no railroad to Murmansk, so the only port open to the sea was Vladivostok on the Pacific! The Allies faced a staggering supply problem shipping weapons around Europe and Asia all the way to Vladivostok, then back by single-track rail on the Trans-Siberian Railroad to Europe. The British tried to break the blockade by seizing the Dardanelles from Turkey, but this effort failed.

Things were getting desperate. So much so that the progressives managed to form a liberal bloc in the Duma to push for reforms. But the government resisted reforms.

What was "the Government" by 1916? This brings us to the story of Rasputin (played in the film by Lionel Barrymore). Rasputin was an evil holy man, a man considered specially blessed by God, who liked to seduce young girls, then forgive them their sin. He explained to them that they could not be in a state of grace unless they had their sins forgiven; and they could not be forgiven until they had committed sin. So he offered both! It was a wonderful line, a package deal – sin and redemption all at once. He was also reputed to have miraculous curative powers and word of this reached the Tsarina Alexandra.

Alexandra was driven to neurosis by the illness of her son, the Tsarevich. He suffered from hemophilia. He was a bleeder. At any moment he might fall and start internal bleeding, or get a cut or have a tooth pulled, all of which threatened death. This was very upsetting to his mother. Before war began, he had a fall and began internal bleeding. And he was in great pain. A lady at the

37

court said she heard of a holy man who could cure people. The distraught Tsarina ordered that he be sent for. He arrived, went into the sick boy's room and behold! the pain and bleeding stopped. The Tsarina was delirious with joy. She embraced Rasputin as a "friend" of the family and he now had ready access to the Court. During the war, while the Tsar was off at the front, Rasputin came to have enormous influence over the Tsarina.

There are many letters from the Tsarina to the Tsar illustrating the influence of Rasputin: "Our friend says appoint so and so to be general of the army." "Our friend says fire so and so." So in effect, "the Government" by the end of 1916 was Rasputin and the Empress! He kept urging resistance to the Duma and rejection of any reforms.

He was, in the eyes of many nobles, a threat to the monarchy. That institution seemed the only thing holding Russia together, and now it was being debased by Rasputin. So a plot was hatched to kill him. He was invited to a party by Prince Yussapov and others in December of 1916. There they fed him poisoned cakes, each with enough poison to kill a regiment. But he did not die. They then gave him poisoned wine, but still he did not die. So then they began to shoot him. He figured the party was over, and started to walk out sloshing with poison and lead! He reached the front steps before he collapsed. The plotters had been mystified. They thought he might be the Anti-Christ. They carried the body to the nearby frozen canal, chopped a hole in the ice and pushed the body down into the water. But he then started to climb out again! They then bashed in his skull with the pick axe they had used to cut the hole in the ice. He finally disappeared. But it was too late. The Imperial Family, the adhesive holding the shattered Russian state together, had been discredited. Now the way was open to Revolution.

8

THE REVOLUTIONS AND CHAOS

There were two revolutions in 1917. Sometimes people forget that and assume the Bolsheviks overthrew the Tsar. That is not true. The Bolsheviks succeeded in overthrowing the only democratic regime Russia ever had, the moderate socialist Provisional Government.

The first Revolution in March was essentially a patriotic uprising of people anxious to win the war. The Tsarist system, trying to cope with fighting, feeding and supplying the Army and the people, had collapsed. There were large-scale desertions in the Army. It is estimated that the entire Russian Army that entered the war had been replaced by 1917. In the cities there were long lines and general griping about the failure of the regime (sound familiar?). By early March spontaneous strikes had begun. On March 9 there was some shooting from rooftops at mobs of demonstrators in St. Petersburg. That day the Duma formed a new government. That same day the Socialists and Communists formed the first "Soviet of Workers and Soldiers". In effect, Russia got two new governments that day. But although the Soviet had the power and popular support, they would not take the responsibility of government. That was left to the Duma.

One of the first acts of the new Duma government was to reassert its determination to carry on the war and stand by its promise to the Allies not to enter into a separate peace. This was a very honorable thing to do but a foolish act since Russia no longer had the strength to carry on the war. On March 16, the Tsar abdicated. The revolution was over! Russia was a republic! And only

169 people had been killed. The same day the Provisional Government was formed, radical groups in St. Petersburg established an unofficial government called the "Soviet" or council. Similar Soviets were formed in other cities.

The Bolsheviks immediately started to plan a counter-revolution to overthrow this fledging democracy. When the March Revolution took place, Bolshevik leaders were out of town. Lenin was in exile in Switzerland. Trotsky was in the United States, and Stalin was in the slammer in Siberia. Lenin returned to Russia in April 1917, with German help. Since the new Russian government was going to continue to fight, Berlin agreed to send in Lenin to overthrow it, like inoculating a disease germ into a body to kill it. The plan was to work well, (except for the final consequences as Soviet troops stormed into Berlin in 1945).

When Lenin arrived in St. Petersburg there was a power vacuum. Suddenly the Bolsheviks got control of the St. Petersburg Soviet. Immediately they shouted a new slogan, "Peace! Bread! Land! All power to the Soviets!" During the night of November 6–7, 1917, the Bolsheviks got control of St. Petersburg. The moderate Socialist leader, Kerensky, was caught completely off guard. (Fifty years later, discussing this, Kerensky commented, "It is difficult to talk about this because it was absolutely against honesty", a revelation of his naivité about the Communists.)

The night they seized power, Bolshevik leaders met in a small room to discuss "What next?" They had plotted for the seizure of power for years. Now, suddenly, they had it. There were only14 or 15 men who met in that room. They did not even have enough to fill all the ministries. When an American, John Reed, walked in someone shouted, "Let's make him Minister of Post and Telegraph!" Lenin was amazed that they had succeeded. He commented that although they now held power, would they be alive the next day? He later said, "It was as easy as picking up a feather!" and further, "It was surprising there was no one there to kick us out right away!"

The next task was to consolidate power by taking control of the Soviets of Moscow and other cities. First it was necessary to neutralize the peasantry, to keep them out of the fight. So Lenin told them to seize the land, that it was theirs to use. Theoretically all land now belonged to the state, but the peasants did not see the subtlety of this. Earlier they had believed all land belonged to God, but they had the use of it. The new decree did not seem to interfere with their seizure of lands of the nobles and church. So they began a land-grab frenzy.

Before its collapse, the Provisional Government had arranged for free elections for a constituent assembly to write a new constitution for the Russian Republic. Many may have been less concerned about the Bolshevik power seizure, feeling that the elections would produce a democratic government for them. The elections were scheduled for late November, too soon for the Bolsheviks to stop them. There were about 42,000,000 votes cast. Of these the Bolsheviks got less than 10,000,000 or about 23 per cent. Of the 704 seats in this freely elected legislature, the Bolsheviks only held 175. The more moderate Social Revolutionaries got 410, enough for a stable majority to construct a new, more moderate government. But the assembly, which met in January 1918, was simply dismissed by the now more powerful Bolsheviks who were strengthening their hold on the nation.

The result would be a civil war incited by the Bolshevik surrender to Germany in 1918. When they seized power, the Bolsheviks claimed a party membership of only 240,000, a tiny minority of the nation. To make consolidation of power possible, they felt it imperative to end the war at almost any cost.

The German price for peace was severe indeed. Russia had to give up vast amounts of territory – Finland, the Baltic States, Poland, the Ukraine, and Trans-Caucasian areas. This meant enormous losses to Russia: over one-third of her population, two-thirds of her industry, three-quarters of her iron production, one-third of her railroad track mileage, nine-tenths of her coal production, etc. It was a catastrophic setback. The Russian people were furious and this was decisive in fueling the Civil War 1918–1921.

The new Soviet regime faced enormous odds: three White armies, and separatist movements in many areas (Ukraine, Baltic States, Finland, Georgia, Armenia, White Russia, and parts of Central Asia). They also faced Allied intervention and occupation of certain ports like Archangel, Batum, Vladivostok, in addition to a war with Poland, and the opposition of the Czech Legion, fighting its way eastward along the Trans-Siberian Railroad to get to the Pacific and on to Europe to continue fighting the Austrians. These seemed impossible odds. Yet by 1922 the Soviets had triumphed. They did not regain everything. They did get back the vital Ukraine, White Russia, the Trans-Caucasian republics and Central Asia. But they lost Finland, the Baltic States and Poland.

The period 1917–1921 was called the Utopian Stage of the Revolution. This Civil War phase, also called the period of "War Communism", saw the Soviet regime move from idealism to stark realism and hard discipline.

Initially the Communists strove for true equality. They wanted to abolish all laws, to do away with the money system, to leap directly into Utopia. But the result was a collapse of the economy. By 1921 industrial production had fallen to 20 per cent of that of 1913. Their Gross National Product was down 87 per cent! Agricultural production had fallen 50 per cent and there was famine in the land.

Lenin told Armand Hammer, the American financier, "It's not working!" Their system was not working. They would have to try something different. And so, in 1921, Lenin introduced his New Economic Policy, or N.E.P., which was a compromise with capitalism. It encouraged individual incentive, something that is missing in any true socialist society. Under N.E.P., an individual could manufacture things for profit if he employed no more than 20 men without a motor or 10 men with a motor. This would prevent the rise of an IBM but would allow for, say, the production of key chains, small vases, frisbees, etc. N.E.P. also decreed that the peasants were to have the land for 99 years. After turning in a small quota to the state at a fixed price, they could sell the rest on the free market for whatever they could get. This was intended to favor "the diligent peasant" and it did. N.E.P. was successful. By 1928 the economy was back to the level of 1913. But then came Stalin.

42

9

STALIN

When the Communists seized power in Russia, they assumed that the Revolution would spread quickly all over the world. This is what Marx had said would happen. Marx had also written that the revolution would begin in the most advanced industrial nations of the world, then spread to the less developed. But Russia was agrarian, not industrial. Nevertheless they had reason for optimism. With the collapse of the Central Powers it looked like Germany might embrace Communism and there seemed nothing to stop the sweep of the Revolution from the Rhine to the Pacific. They pushed for revolution in Germany, in Hungary, in Poland, China and other areas during the 1920s. But when the dust had settled by the mid-1920s the only other nation to embrace communism was Outer Mongolia, and that could hardly be called an advanced industrial state when the people there were still living in yurts.

Lenin died in 1924 (30 years too late) and a power struggle began between two of his chief lieutenants, Leon Trotsky and Josef Stalin. Lenin had serious reservations about Stalin but had not designated an heir. Stalin was able to outmaneuver Trotsky. Stalin was Secretary of the Communist Party and as such controlled party appointments and machinery, and the party controlled Russia. Trotsky had argued for continuing to foster revolutions overseas, believing it impossible for Communist Russia to survive in a hostile, capitalist world. Yet all their revolutionary activity was backfiring. By pushing Communist revolution in Hungary, Poland, Germany and China they simply strengthened the forces of reaction and nationalism in those countries. And

Communist plots in places like England and France and America simply made more enemies.

Trotsky encouraged international revolutionary efforts under the direction of the Comintern (Communist International). He was discredited as these efforts failed. By 1927 he had been exiled, and Stalin was firmly in control.

Who was Stalin? Trotsky called him "an outstanding mediocrity". He was relatively short, five feet four inches tall, with a left arm three inches shorter than the right (a malady also shared by Kaiser Wilhelm of Germany). He was born in Georgia, and his name was Josef Vissarianovich Dzhugashvili. He changed it to "Stalin" (thank goodness), which meant "steel". The name suited him. His father was a cobbler who drank too much and beat his son. His mother was a simple peasant who wanted her son to become a priest! He did attend a seminary but was expelled after six years. (The world should condemn the Dean of Boys responsible for having unleashed a monster. The same charge could be made for the Dean of Admissions at the Vienna Art Academy who would not let Hitler become a third-rate artist. History should condemn these tough administrators!) After his expulsion, Stalin became a revolutionary and was known by the police as "a coarse and brutal man". By 1922 Stalin had become General Secretary of the Communist Party and as such controlled the Party and the state.

In 1927 Stalin outlined his immediate objective. It was based on the principle of "Socialism in one Country". Stalin believed they should tone down international revolutionary activity because they were simply intensifying the antagonism of the West. Russia would not be able to face a conflict with the capitalist powers until they had military power. And they could not have an effective military until they had a powerful industrial base. So the priorities were first to industrialize the nation, then build up its military power, then face the inevitable conflicts with the West that Lenin had predicted.

Stalin also outlined his long-range international strategy in 1927 in a series of lectures at Sverdlovsk. Instead of fighting bourgeois nationalists in various areas of the world, the Communists must ally with them. He took Lenin's theory of imperialism one step further. Lenin had argued that things had improved for workers in the West because the capitalists had expanded their exploitation to the masses of Asia and Africa and could therefore afford to drop a few crumbs to their own workers. This was the new "Stage of Imperialism" that Lenin declared was the dying stage of capitalism. In time the masses of the colonial regions would rise up against their masters and the collapse of world capitalist imperialism would begin. In the meantime, Stalin argued, Communists were to ally with progressive forces of bourgeois nationalism to throw out the imperialists. Once this was done, the Communists would purge the non-Communists from the new government and proclaim a Communist state. This strategy worked brilliantly later on in places like China and Viet Nam where the Communists became the champions of nationalism (a force they really opposed). The theory went on that once the colonial areas were free, the Western industrial powers would lapse into incipient depression and would end up in desperation anxiously embracing Communism.

Parenthetically, this strategy was carried one step further in the 1960s by Mao Tse Tung's number two man (until he was liquidated) Lin Piao. Lin noted how brilliantly Mao had communized the countryside of China against the cities. The poor peasants had been drawn to this cause long before the urban areas of China. When the Communists moved to take over all of China they had already controlled the countryside in the north. The Nationalists only held the cities and the rail lines between those cities. So the control of the Nationalists' leader, Chiang Kai-shek, resembled soft strands of spaghetti strewn on a cloth of black velvet. The Communists only had to snip the rail lines and the collapse of nationalist China followed quickly. Lin proclaimed that just as Mao had mobilized the countryside of China against the cities, so now would Mao's China mobilize the world countryside (Asia, Africa, Latin America) against the World City – that industrial complex straddling the Atlantic. It was a majestic strategy.

Stalin was to transform Russia and drag that nation into one of the most dismal periods of her history through his determination to industrialize and mobilize the nation behind him.

He would subject Russia to a 25-year reign of terror from 1929 to his death in 1953. Authorities are still uncovering mass graves and adding millions to the roster of those killed or exiled under his tyranny.

Stalin was determined to industrialize Russia at any cost so that the country could face the industrialized, capitalist world. He used forced collectivization to achieve this by ruthlessly evicting millions of peasants from farms to new industrial cities and collectivizing agriculture. In 1931 he told a group of managers, "We are 50 or 100 years behind the advanced countries. We must make good this lag in 10 years". Again the catch-up theme of Russian history was revived, which has recurred periodically ever since the 17th century.

The collectivization of agriculture was carried on in a brutal fashion. (The best account of this is Robert Conquest's book, *Harvest of Sorrow*.) Stalin was determined to destroy the rich peasant class, whom Lenin had encouraged, and who were now labeled "Kulaks". They must turn in all their livestock and farm equipment to the collective or be exiled or killed. Millions would die. Millions!

The Party began to force peasants into collectives in 1929. The pressure was intensified during the next few years. From 1932 to 1934 the Party created a man-made famine. They staked out a huge area of rich farmland with its prosperous farmers, and deliberately starved them. No one was to hoard food, not even seed grain for the coming year. Stalin later said that 10 million had died in this affair. More reliable estimates put the figure at 10 to 20 million. Another 25 million people were forcibly moved to new industrial areas.

Some 25 million private farms (in 1929) were converted to about 100,000 collective farms. In the process over half the horses and livestock were gone. Peasants had eaten them figuring they may as well enter the collective naked. Soviet meat and butter production never fully recovered from this catastrophic loss.

By 1934 Soviet agricultural production was 35 per cent below that of 1913! And there were millions more mouths to feed. In 1935 Stalin agreed to a slight compromise. Each peasant household was to be allowed a small private plot, a little over one acre. Whatever was raised on that plot could be sold on the free market.

This allowed a tiny bit of private incentive and it worked. By 1937 agricultural production was back to 95 per cent of 1913.

The contrast between the production per square foot on the private plots and that of the collectives has always been remarkable. During the 1960s the private plots, only 3 per cent of the land of the USSR, were producing about 35 per cent of the food! This meant the collectives, 97 per cent of the land, were producing only about 65 per cent of the food. Today the private plots must be producing at least 50 per cent of the food.

I heard of one case where a farmer from Tashkent was able to fly over 2,000 miles to Moscow with a bag of melons, sell them, and return home with a profit! This was not only because of the high price of the melons, but also due to the low state-subsidized air fare from Tashkent to Moscow. (I flew that in 1990 and the fare was only $60. In America it would be about $300.)

The horrors of Stalin's forced collectivization were followed by the horrors of his purges from 1934 to 1938. The latest figures are that over seven million people were condemned to death, ten times the KGB figure announced as recently as 1990. And, of course, millions more died from the dreadful conditions of the slave labor camps.

The purges began in 1934 after the assassination of Sergei Kirov, Stalin's man in Leningrad, who was probably killed on Stalin's orders. Some eight to twelve million were arrested, including one-fourth of the total population of Leningrad. Slave labor camps all over Russia were filled. At least two million died and they are still finding new mass graves. The final figure will never be known.

Khrushchev later reported that some 383 death lists had been issued just during 1937 and 1938. Over one million Party members were liquidated. According to Khrushchev, of the nearly 2,000 delegates to the 1934 Party Congress, only 59 were left by the time of the next Party Congress in 1939. Of 139 Central Committee members, 98 were shot. After Khrushchev had recounted all of this at the meeting he accepted written questions from the floor. One of these was, "If Stalin was such a butcher in the 1930s and 40s what were YOU doing in his inner circle all that time?" Khrushchev shouted back, "WHO SENT THAT QUESTION??"

Silence. Then Khrushchev said, "That's what I was doing" (suffering years of frozen, silent terror).

The Red Army was purged down to the level of Captain. Three of the five marshals were killed, 11 out of 15 Army commanders, 62 out of 80 corps commanders, all eight admirals, etc. This left young inexperienced officers to face the Germans in World War II. The weakness of the Red Army was clearly revealed in 1939 when it took on tiny Finland and needed several months to defeat it.

According to a current Russian school text, some 40 to 50 million people died because of Stalin: some 20 to 30 million in the collectivization crisis plus some 20 million from purges and terror. The Soviet Union became a personal despotism under Stalin. Writers and artists were to follow the dictates of "Socialist Realism". No abstract art, just paintings of machinery or leaders, composition only of music to plow by, etc. A recent film, *The Inner Circle*, hints at the terror of this period under Stalin.

10

WORLD WAR II

During the drab and frightening 1930s, the Soviet Union felt isolated and in serious danger as Germany, Italy and Japan drew together in a coalition while the Western democracies continually retreated before aggression in Manchuria, the Rhineland, Austria and Czechoslovakia. The Soviets were also alarmed at the Maginot-Line mentality of the French, which assumed that if the Germans attacked to the East, the French would simply huddle in their famed Maginot Line playing ping pong, watching movies, reading girlie magazines and taking sun-lamp treatments until the Germans had exhausted themselves slaughtering Slavs. This was not a happy prospect for the Soviets.

And so the Soviets began to extend feelers toward Germany in the spring of 1939 for a new understanding. They did not want to face a war if at all possible. They would like to avoid it, which seemed feasible since German actions seemed to threaten Anglo-French policy more than Soviet. By the spring of 1939 the Western Powers had finally taken a firm stand against Hitler. If he attacked Poland, Britain and France would fight. Hitler made his final decision in May to attack Poland by the end of summer 1939. Britain, France and Germany were now committed. The Western Powers thereby lost all their freedom of action, but not Stalin. He would play his hand very skillfully.

In April the Soviet representative in Berlin extended an offer of good political relations between Germany and the USSR despite their ideological differences. Hitler decided to respond to this overture. If the British and French really wanted to save Poland, they could not do so without the aid of the USSR. If Hitler could get the Soviets to agree to remain neutral, then the West could do nothing for Poland. Therefore, being logical people, they would not fight and Hitler could have a quick local war to conquer Poland.

The Soviets dragged their feet during the negotiations while also entertaining the possibility of an alliance with Britain and France if things did not work out with Berlin. Stalin was wary of Hitler who had been hurling obscenities at him for a decade. From May to August Stalin engaged in long, drawn-out negotiations with both sides. And why not? He still had his freedom of action while the other players were frozen in their positions. While he negotiated with both sides, he obviously preferred a deal with Hitler because Hitler could offer him a period of peace and a slice of Eastern Europe while the West could only offer him war, and war at a disadvantage.

The slow pace of the negotiations frustrated the Germans who were planning to attack Poland at the end of August. Finally, at the end of July, German negotiators took their Soviet counterparts out to dinner at a Berlin restaurant. The Germans pointed out that relations with Poland were near a breaking point, but that there were no conflicts between Germany and the USSR anywhere along the line from the Baltic to the Black Sea. The Soviet dinner guests then mentioned various parts of Eastern Europe – eastern Poland, the Baltic States, parts of Romania. In each instance the Germans repeated the phrase that there were "no conflicts anywhere along the line from the Baltic to the Black Sea". The point was made.

Stalin now agreed to a non-aggression pact. He suggested that Ribbentrop come to Moscow in a couple of weeks, not realizing Hitler's timetable. Hitler replied, "How about tomorrow?" Stalin was a bit thrown by this. Among other things it is difficult to get a hotel room in Moscow with soap, etc. at short notice. And he would have to explain to loyal Communist fanatics all over the world why he was dealing with the devil. He finally agreed to Ribbentrop coming in a couple of days.

Ribbentrop arrived in Moscow on August 20 and began the negotiations. Stalin wanted a "sphere" over Finland, half of Poland, a slice of Romania, Estonia and Latvia. Ribbentrop asked,

"All of Latvia?" Evidently Hitler anticipated getting half – the Libau area. So Ribbentrop asked for a brief recess, phoned Hitler at Berchtesgaden reporting that Stalin wanted all of Latvia. Hitler put the phone down, went over to the atlas in the corner of his office, found Latvia and said simply, "Yes, agreed". And in that one moment Latvia went down the toilet for 50 years. Stalin had no idea how frantic Hitler was for the quick conclusion of this agreement. If Stalin had asked, Ribbentrop had instructions to allot him the Balkans, down to and including the Dardanelles!

The Nazi-Soviet Non-Aggression Pact was announced to the world on August 22. The news shocked the world. It would be like finding Hillary Clinton in a love nest with Rush Limbaugh.

Hitler assumed the British and French would now give up the idea that they could help Poland. But he was wrong. When Germany attacked Poland, the Allies stood by the Poles. A few days later Stalin stood by his commitments in the Pact. He got a sphere over much of Eastern Europe. Since the Germans had occupied more of Poland than was planned, Hitler tossed Lithuania into Stalin's basket. It had been intended for Germany. Now it would languish under Soviet tyranny for 50 years.

While Stalin seized his allotted share of Eastern Europe (except for the problem of Finland), he maintained good relations with Hitler. The Soviet Union exported to Germany all the grain, oil, etc. for which they were asked. The Communist Party in France was ordered to spread defeatism. Party fanatics in America were ordered to foster isolationism, to keep America out of this "dirty capitalist war".

In the fall of 1940, France collapsed. This was totally unexpected by the British, the Americans, certainly by the French, and also by the Soviets. Stalin had assumed the German Army would bog down in France as they had in World War I. Now suddenly Stalin was faced with the horrifying prospect of being alone with Hitler on the continent of Europe. Could they work out another division of spheres to avoid future conflict? For this purpose the Soviet Foreign Minister Molotov was invited to Berlin.

There followed in November 1940 a rather obscene conference. Hitler was proposing to divide the Eurasian world among the Germans, Italians, Russians and Japanese, in such a way that they would not collide. Molotov evidently had instructions to ask for another piece of Romania, a base in the Dardanelles, and perhaps one governing the entry to the Baltic. Hitler opened the meeting by presenting his majestic mural of a partitioned world. Japan would expand south toward southeast Asia. Italy would expand south further into the Sahara Desert. Germany would expand southeast toward the Near East. Russia would expand south toward the Persian Gulf. That way, with all four expanding parallel and southward, they would not collide with one another. Molotov countered asking for a base in the Dardanelles. Hitler told him to forget that. It was this Russian drive to the southwest that collided with Germany's drive to the southeast and caused World War I. The Soviet Union's destiny lay to the south, he said, toward the Persian Gulf where they would find very warm-water ports. He offered Iran to Russia. Molotov hesitated, probably checking his notes about bits and pieces of East Europe. Hitler then offered Russia Afghanistan. Molotov must have been impressed. He may have said – "Wow! How do you spell that?" But there was no mention of Afghanistan in his instructions from Stalin and no Russian in his right mind would think independently of Stalin. Molotov then asked for a piece of Bukovina, a province of Romania. Hitler became exasperated and must have said something to the effect: "Molotov! Bukovina Smukovina. Think big! Do you want India? All India? It's yours! And nowhere can you find warmer ports than in India!" But Molotov did not respond. He must have made notes; but he was not able to discuss such things. He was a political birdseed counter. He said he would report all this to Stalin. Hitler then broke off the discussions, told Molotov not to call him that he would call Molotov.

After this conference Hitler decided he could not trust the Soviets. They still entertained traditional Tsarist ambitions of expansion to the southwest, toward the Dardenelles. This would collide with German objectives. And he dared not extend his drive through the Balkans and across Egypt towards the Suez Canal and the oil riches of the Middle East while Soviet power threatened his eastern flank. He dared not overextend until the Soviet Union had been smashed.

He made his decision in December 1940 to attack the Soviets.

The Americans and British found out about this through diligent spy work and warned Stalin. But he suspected an imperialist trick and would not believe the reports. He went on collaborating with Hitler.

The day the Germans attacked Russia, June 21, 1941, Churchill was in the House of Commons with a speech all prepared welcoming the Soviets as allies. That same day there were Communist pickets in front of the White House urging America to stay out of this "dirty imperialist war". Someone drove up in a car, whispered the news to the picketers. They threw their placards into the car and drove off. The very next day they were out there again with new signs, "Help the Brave Democracies in Their Struggle Against Hitlerite Aggression!"

Stalin was reportedly staggered by the German attack. He was on vacation in the Crimea. According to Khrushchev, he was drunk for four days. They had to sober him up and bring him to Moscow to lead. Meanwhile the German tide moved eastward. Quickly overrunning the Baltic States and the Ukraine, areas which first welcomed the Germans as liberators, Hitler's forces marched to within sight of Moscow; but they did not quite make it.

One reason for this was a spy story in Tokyo. The Soviets had a spy, Richard Sorge, in the German Embassy in Japan. He found out in the fall of 1941 that the Japanese were going to strike south rather than to the north. Hitler had been urging the Japanese to attack Russia, telling them that the Red Army had been crushed. But the Japanese concluded, if Russia is beaten, why bother? Besides, if they struck south they could get access to the rich sources of oil, rubber, tin and other critical commodities of war that the Americans had stopped sending. If they struck north, all they would find would be cabbages and cucumbers. So they struck south hitting Pearl Harbor in the process. Now Stalin knew this was going to happen; but he did not tell the US. Instead he used his information from Sorge to move most of his troops from the Manchurian border to the defense of Moscow. Sorge later claimed he was the one who saved Moscow. And there is much evidence to support him.

With the Pearl Harbor attack, the war had become a truly global one. The Axis Powers almost succeeded, but they did not quite make it. The Germans tried a gigantic enveloping movement to conquer the entire Middle East in 1942. Their forces in Russia would pour south over the Caucasus toward Iran while Rommel would move across North Africa to Suez. As soon as they were close, the Arabs would rise up in Syria, Iraq and even Palestine, to install pro-Axis governments and join with Hitler. The Iranians would also change their government and join the Axis. Then Germany would have all the oil it needed, the Suez Canal would be closed and the only countries separating the Germans from the Japanese would be an unreliable India (which might throw out the British and join Japan), and a broken Russia on the verge of collapse. In 1942 they came very very close. It was the high-watermark for the Axis and almost brought catastrophe to the Allies.

But the Germans did not quite make it. While the Japanese were stopped in the Pacific by forces led by John Wayne and Kirk Douglas, the Germans were stopped at the Battle of El Alemein in Egypt and the titanic Battle of Stalingrad in Russia. From the end of 1942 until 1945 the war was a story of almost uninterrupted Allied advance and Axis retreat.

But as one war was winding down, the next, the "Cold War" was being started (heating up?).

11

THE COLD WAR

The roots of the Cold War can be traced back deep into the nightmare of World War II. The basic problem was that the alliance of Britain, the Soviet Union and the United States was an involuntary one. In fact it was downright unnatural. Imagine as bedfellows imperialist Britain, Communist Russia, and naively liberal United States. The only one to enter the war voluntarily was Britain. The Soviet Union was only drawn in when Hitler attacked them. And the United States was forced in by Japan.

Could these three odd characters get along in molding the peace after the war? What kind of world did each want? To sound out the Soviets on this, the British Foreign Secretary, Anthony Eden, went to Moscow in December 1941. He wanted to get some idea of Stalin's war aims. He was shaken by Stalin's answer. Stalin pointed out that at the very minimum the Soviets would keep the advanced frontiers to which Hitler had agreed. In other words, Russia would hang on to the Baltic States and half of Poland, which shot down the pro-Soviet argument that Stalin did not really want to keep these but had only taken them for advance defense against a future German attack. Beyond this, Stalin was determined to maintain control of all Eastern Europe as a sphere of control. He suggested that Britain establish a sphere of influence over Western Europe, to be guaranteed by Britain seizing bases in France, the Netherlands, Norway, etc. In between these two spheres would be a broken Germany, which would be kept perpetually weak through heavy reparations. Stalin would agree to cut Germany down to any size Britain wanted, giving chunks to

55

France, the Low Countries, Denmark and Poland.

Anthony Eden was stunned. These proposals were at complete variance with British war aims. Britain had gone to war to rescue Poland, to reestablish a balance of power in Europe, and to preserve her empire. Stalin was proposing to divide Europe into spheres with a dead Germany to the center. What Stalin sought would mean the end of Europe. So Eden could not even discuss these proposals. He could only engage in small talk ("Nice Kremlin you have here. Cold isn't it?")

Then the United States jumped into the fray with the enthusiasm and idealism of a Boy Scout. Franklin Roosevelt outlined his vision of a postwar world in his speech on the Four Freedoms in January 1941. He wanted a world in which everyone would enjoy freedom of speech, freedom of religion, freedom from fear, and freedom from want. In other words, a world in which there would be peace, freedom and prosperity for all. Of course these objectives would threaten both the Soviet and the British Empires.

The Allies set these conflicts aside for the time being, the major problem being to win the war. But these festered in the background, especially the Polish question because Britain was committed to restore Poland; and the large Polish-American voting block was dedicated to the same thing. American political party platforms during the war called for the restoration of Poland with her prewar frontiers. This conflict was bound to well up to the surface.

The first major disturbance in the alliance came about when the Germans found a mass grave of Polish officers, thousands of them, methodically executed by the Soviets before the area was occupied by the Germans. This was the infamous Katyn Forest Massacre. Of course the idea of the Germans protesting about an atrocity at that time would be like Catherine the Great objecting to nude paintings in the Sistine Chapel. Nevertheless the Germans pursued it by inviting Red Cross officials to investigate. And although the Soviets denied it, the evidence proved they did indeed shoot some 15,000 Polish officers because they represented the educated upper class which might threaten Soviet control of Poland one day.

The Russian government finally admitted to the deed in April

1990 and the newly independent Poland could issue a stamp remembering the victims of Katyn. Today the Poles are still finding mass graves of those executed under Stalin's orders in his fanatical determination to control their country. A mass grave was discovered near Bialostok in 1989 containing the bodies of hundreds of Polish underground fighters who were helping the Allied cause. After the area was liberated the Soviets asked all underground fighters to report. They did so thinking they were to carry on the fight. Instead they disappeared. This must have happened all over Eastern Europe as Stalin brutally wiped out anyone who might threaten Soviet control.

The most infamous evidence of this was the uprising of the Warsaw Underground in the summer of 1944. The Red Army was approaching the city. The Polish Government in exile in London wanted their capital city liberated by the Poles. So they rose up and seized control of the city from the Germans. Then the Germans began to counter-attack. The Poles asked the Red Army to enter. They were just across the river. But the Soviets replied with regrets that they could not, that they lacked sufficient fuel! They had had enough to advance 1,000 miles from Stalingrad to the suburbs of Warsaw but could not go the extra mile. Obviously Stalin was going to let the Germans do his dirty work. They would annihilate the nationalistic Polish Underground, then the Soviets would occupy a prostrate Poland. The Poles appealed to the West for help. America asked the Soviets that if they flew shuttle supply planes over Warsaw and air dropped supplies could they refuel in Russia. The Soviets refused, which made their true objective very clear. The brave resistance in Warsaw collapsed.

At this point, the London Polish Government-in-Exile broke off relations with the Soviet Union. The Soviet response was to set up a puppet Communist government in Lublin, in their occupied part of Poland. There were now two Polish Governments, the London Poles and the Lublin Poles. This exposed a real split within the Allied coalition. Something had to be done. Certain problems of the peace could no longer be postponed. The result was the Yalta Conference in February 1945.

The central problem at Yalta was the Polish question. The Big Three reached a compromise. Poland was picked up and moved about 150 miles to the west. Russia was to keep the eastern half that Hitler had allowed. As compensation Poland was to receive about one-fifth of prewar Germany. The two Polish governments were to be combined, the conservative peasant government in London and the puppet Communist regime in Lublin. This is like putting mustard on ice cream. The London Premier was to be the new overall Premier, but the Communists kept the key Ministry of the Interior, which controlled areas of government that included the police, the election procedures and education. In other words it really controlled the country.

The Powers also agreed that there were to be "free and unfettered democratic elections" in Eastern Europe after the war. America considered this a victory since it was obvious the Soviets would have occupied the area anyway. Stalin also promised to join the US in the Pacific war, (for which I was personally grateful since I was a young draftee at the time, slated for the invasion of the Japanese home islands, an invasion in which we expected at least one million casualties on both sides. So I was grateful for any help we could get).

The war in Europe ended in May 1945. It had produced tremendous losses for Russia, the latest estimates are as many as 29 million killed. This was the third demographic catastrophe in Soviet history. After the famines of 1921 and 1931, after the purges and terrors of the 1930s, and after the losses of the war the Soviet population was some 50 million less than it should have been. In other words, at least 50 million people were not there in 1945 who should have been.

The war was followed by a new demographic terror by Stalin. Millions of peoples were deported to the interior of Siberia – those considered disloyal during the war including Baltic peoples, Germans, Tatars, Jews and Poles. Stalin said he wanted to deport all the Ukrainians too but there were too many of them!

Adding these atrocities to the millions of others killed by Stalin in purges and terror qualifies Stalin for the title of "butcher" conferred upon him by Khrushchev. Hitler was possibly the worst thing to happen to our century, but Stalin was far worse than Hitler!

Through the war, Stalin had created a Soviet empire stretching from the Elbe River to the Pacific. Before the war, Chamberlain was anxious to appease Hitler to avoid war if possible by reasonable compromise. He often said that if Germany and England went to war, the only victor would be Bolshevism. By 1945 Stalin would agree.

The United States tried collaboration with Stalin to restore Europe after the war, but got nowhere. Reluctant to abandon the Continent, and refusing to consider a "preventive war", the US adopted the policy of "Containment" which endured from 1947 to 1975. The Marshall Plan and the NATO Alliance helped enormously in the revival of Western Europe. The Soviet response was to consolidate its hold on Eastern Europe by removing non-Communist elements and coalition governments in, for example, Poland, Hungary and Czechoslovakia. The only Communist to resist this final Soviet move to control was Marshall Tito of Yugoslavia. He broke with Stalin and became a Communist heretic, a most significant event. Nationalism was beginning to raise its head within the Soviet bloc. Where and when would this end? (We did not realize it would take 40 years!)

12

AFTER STALIN

Stalin died about 50 years too late. His end involved political drama as thick as any in his monstrous career. By 1953 Stalin had established what later was condemned as a "personality cult" where he was considered to be, for example, the greatest leader, the greatest military strategist, the greatest party theoretician and the greatest art critic. Thousands of geographic places were named after him including cities, mountains and streets. There were over 10,000 statues of him, which were later torn down (which was easy since they were so cheaply made).

But by 1953, according to close observers (especially Khrushchev), Stalin had become "sickly suspicious" of those around him. He was afraid of a Zionist "Doctors' Plot" to poison him. He evidently had been given some pretty awful medicine. The "plot" was announced in the press and nine Kremlin doctors were arrested. Many others simply disappeared. Even some drug stores were closed. The members of the Politburo were terrified for fear that a new purge was about to start.

The following account is from the recollections of Khrushchev. According to him, on February 25, 1953, Stalin collapsed on the floor of his Kremlin office. Other Politburo members were present. It looked like a fatal stroke. Beria, the Secret Police Chief, got quite excited and reportedly danced about crying "Comrades! The old tyrant is dead! We need no longer fear for our lives! Comrades! What a glorious day!" Then Stalin opened his eyes. Beria fell on his knees in abject apologies assuring Stalin he had not meant it, that he was loyal and that the Devil made him say it. Then Stalin closed his eyes again.

The others stood about, silently for a quite a while. Then one said, "I suppose we should call a doctor". Another period of silence. Then someone may have remarked, "I wonder if we should call or write a letter?" More silence. They were in no hurry to rush a cure. When they finally did call a doctor and he found out who the patient was, he refused to come alone. And who can blame him? Doctors were disappearing all around Moscow and they wanted him to treat Stalin?

Finally, after two days, three doctors went in. It was too late. Stalin descended to his reward at the age of 73 on March 5, 1953. Despite all the horrors of the Stalin era there was massive frenzied mourning for him! Some 1,500 mourners were crushed to death at his funeral. He was ceremoniously entombed with Lenin in the downtown mausoleum.

Now the Soviet Union was faced with a serious succession problem. All the really able people had been purged. There were only compliant mediocrities left. Fearful of a new Stalin, the Politburo decided on a triumverate to govern consisting of Malenkov, Molotov, and Kaganovich, with Malenkov as Premier and Party Secretary.

Soon after the news of Stalin's death hit Eastern Europe there was rioting in Poland and East Germany. The cry was spreading throughout the Red Empire that the wicked demon of the East was dead. Then there was reportedly a plot by the KGB Chief, Beria, to seize power. He evidently was suffering from delusions of adequacy and began placing his supporters in key positions. So the others had him shot and his body smuggled out of the Kremlin. The armed forces of the KGB were then disarmed, "not without bloodshed" according to Khrushchev.

At this point a new star began to rise in the Communist horizon, named Nikita Khrushchev. He began to throw his weight around, which was considerable. Two weeks after the death of Stalin, Khrushchev was quietly made Party Secretary, the key position from which Stalin had risen to despotism. But most people thought that Malenkov, the new Premier, was still the major leader.

Khrushchev began to build up his support. His greatest pitch for

Party popularity was in 1956 at the Twentieth Party Congress. There he denounced Stalin as "a tyrant, a butcher, and a murderer". Quite a comedown for the former deity. Stalin's body was transferred from the Tomb to a nitch in the Kremlin Wall. And his statues and place names started to disappear.

This all pushed the USSR into intellectual disarray. In 1957 the Soviet Government had hailed the achievements of Soviet physics in launching Sputnik. But that was also the year Pasternak completed *Dr. Zhivago*, which was testimony to the bankruptcy of Soviet ideology. Pasternak declared that the Bolshevik Revolution was simply a conspiracy of professional revolutionaries and that the only hope for Russia lay in a return to God! Solzhenitsyn then wrote a work comparing the building of socialism to the construction of a prison camp. He commented, "We did it all ourselves, to ourselves". Soviet history had to be rewritten leading to a Polish joke that under Communism "only the future is certain, the past is always changing".

In 1957 Khrushchev paid a visit to Finland. While he was there, the Malenkov faction in the Politburo voted him out of office seven to four. When Khrushchev returned, he said, "Seven to four is arithmetic, gentlemen; it is not politics". It seems that the Politburo could not decide its own membership. The Party Constitution decreed that only the Central Committee could do so, a group of about 125 at that time.

So it was agreed to convene the Central Committee the following Monday. Over the weekend, Khrushchev got on the phone. He made sure all his supporters were coming to the meeting, some as far away as Vladivostok. Malenkov supporters probably got no such timely notice. On Monday the Central Committee met. The Malenkov–Molotov–Kaganovich faction proposed ousting Khrushchev. Motion defeated! Then the Khrushchev group proposed ousting Malenkov, Molotov and Kaganovich. Passed!

The outcasts were not killed, as was the custom in Stalin's day. Instead, their personnel files were examined to see what skills they possessed. Malenkov had once managed a power plant, so he was sent to one in Kazakstan. Kaganovich had once been a factory manager; so they found one for him in Siberia. Molotov had diplomatic experience, so they made him Ambassador to Outer Mongolia.

Although Khrushchev was quite firmly in control, the Soviet Union began to sink into the abyss of pessimism. While anti-Soviet books could not be published, mimeographed manuscripts could be circulated for opinions. And Russia was flooded with this *samizdat* literature. The birth rate was declining. The abortion rate was high. The divorce rate reached 50 per cent, as bad as in the USA. Living standards were increasingly depressed. The Soviet Union seemed to be going nowhere. There were over 40 million registered alcoholics, one of the few emotional outlets left. Rioting broke out afresh in Poland and Hungary in 1956. There was a raising conflict with Communist China.

Khrushchev tried to downplay Utopian themes. He presented what came to be called "Goulash Communism". Speaking to Hungarian workers after having crushed their revolution, he argued that they were not interested so much in ideologies as in "good goulash, schools, housing and ballet". If you omit ballet, this sounds a lot like Herbert Hoover in 1932. Khrushchev boasted that the USSR would surpass the USA in production by the 1970s, then the 1980s, then he stopped giving dates.

He was ousted in 1964 to be replaced by Leonid Brezhnev. This began what the Soviets later condemned as their 21-year "era of stagnation". Brezhnev stressed armaments, to keep up with the USA. He ignored the domestic economy and the growing severe pollution problems caused by reckless industrialization. Brezhnev died in 1982 after 18 years of masterly incompetence and was blamed for the mess the USSR was in the 1980s. He was replaced by a reformer named Yuri Andropov. Andropov was 68 when he was appointed and hoped that Mikhail Gorbachev, another reformer, would be his successor. But, after only two years Andropov died. Hardliners in the Politburo prevailed and another party conservative, Konstantine Chernenko, was appointed at the age of 74. He only lasted a year, 1984–85 when he finally had the decency to die and clear the way for Gorbachev.

The Gorbachev era 1985–1991 was dazzling with its profound changes. He would introduce the world to new terms like *glasnost* meaning openness or truth; *perestroika* meaning reform, restructuring, democracy; *uskorenie* which encompassed a whole range of reforming activity including acceleration, modernization of the economy, introducing more responsibility at the local level, decentralizing decision-making, encouraging more worker incentives, and producing more consumer goods.

Gorbachev concluded at the outset that the system was about to collapse. He learned this from the KGB, the only group which knew what was going on in the USSR. He evidently had alarming reports from KGB officials all over the Soviet Union warning of imminent failure. (Reminds one of the state of Russia in 1905.) Gorbachev commented, "Our people cannot go on living like this!" Some 45 per cent of the Soviet people were reported to live below the poverty line. He reported that their system had failed, that the USSR was getting nowhere, that they needed a new system (just what Lenin had concluded 70 years earlier!). He noted that the USSR was far behind the industrial countries of the world and that it was getting worse. Again the rush to catch up reappeared.

The most crucial element needed for success was to introduce incentive into Soviet life. This has been the major drawback of Soviet and other Communist societies where centralized control means that no one seems to give a damn. There is no interest in doing good work or working hard. You are paid the same. So both the quantity and quality of nearly everything in the Soviet Union is poor.

There is a critical problem in the food supply system (again like the last years of the Tsars). It is estimated that 40 per cent of the food supply does not reach the market. It either rots in the fields or on railroad sidings waiting for trains that never arrive. Senator Moynihan commented at the time that in this highly complex computerized world, the Soviet Union is still "peddling fish, eggs and furs, the trading goods of a hunter-gatherer economy".

In 1991 a Soviet public opinion survey asked, "What does the Soviet Union offer its citizens?" Over 65 per cent replied, "shortages, waiting in lines, and a miserable existence".

The Soviet system had become fossilized. Trying to manage a modern industrial state according to the teachings of Marxism is like trying to run the IBM Corporation according to the Farmers' Almanac.

Gorbachev was too fast for some, too slow for others. In August

1991 Party hardliners attempted another coup by establishing what they called "The State Committee for the State of Emergency". Army tanks moved into Moscow on August 19; there was a standoff on August 20, and the nerves of the coup leaders began to crack. Gorbachev was able to return to Moscow from vacation on August 21, but his popularity had weakened and was overshadowed by that of Boris Yeltsin, the hero of the resistance whose supporters held out in the Russian White House armed with a fax machine and fortified with two truckloads of sausage and two truckloads of pizza from Pizza Hut.

Yeltsin had built his power base on the Russian Republic, not the USSR. The Soviet Union came to an end under Yeltsin's attack. This ended the career of Mikhael Gorbachev who had built his power base on the USSR. When the 15 republics, including Russia, left the Soviet Union, Gorbachev was only left in command of his office suite. So he resigned.

Yeltsin wanted to bundle the former Soviet Republics into a loose confederation known as "The Commonwealth of Independent States". But only 3 of the former 15 republics joined (Russia, The Ukraine, and Belorus). And ethnic tensions threatened the stability of that union.

There were over 100 restless minorities within the former Soviet Union. The Russians were actually a minority (see map page 66). And nationalist tensions continue to threaten the Russian Republic (for example, Chechens, Ossetians and Tatars). Only about half the Russian Republic is inhabited by Russians! The rest of its area consists of autonomous republics, regions, and districts (see map page 66).

Russia today reminds me of Russia in 1905. There are food shortages, political and ethnic tensions and the ever-present threat of another coup. Or there could be a spontaneous general strike, like that of 1905 when the people had just had enough.

Certain crucial abilities must be revived in Russia after 70 years of Communist depression. The first is the ability to work hard, to put in an honest day's work. The Soviet system suffered from overemployment, hiring ten people to do the work of about six, for example, so that many workers labored sporadically or sat around with little to do. No one was in a hurry.

How Russian is Russia?

- Soviet Republics
- Autonomous areas of the Russian Republic
- The Russian part of the Russian Republic

Russians in USSR

Second, the Russians must relearn the importance of quality work. There was no incentive to work well under Communism. But with the rise of competition in labor, and the entry of Russia into the competitive open world-market they need to do good work. And good work must be rewarded. Poor work must no longer be tolerated.

Things are slowly changing. The Russian people are regaining their warm humor. They are learning to smile again. Young trainees at McDonalds, Kentucky Fried Chicken, Pizza Hut, Baskin & Robbins Ice Cream and other foreign firms are learning to be courteous and are becoming accustomed to hard work. Foreign firms are building or rebuilding hotels. The staff are learning how to keep them clean and maintain a happy attitude, so different from the Soviet style of dismal, dirty, defiant and depressing service.

They also need to relearn how to take initiative, instead of waiting for decisions on even minor matters by superiors. And individual incentive needs to be encouraged not discouraged.

I was driving with a busload of desperate tourists in 1996 across Kazakhstan in search of a toilet. There are very few between cities. I commented to the guide that I ought to start a chain of public toilets charging 50 kopeks per usage. The guide immediately snapped back, "Where are you going to get the toilets? You must import them. You will need an import license. You will also need foreign exchange to buy them. How will you get permission for that? And where are you going to get toilet paper? Then you will need construction permits to build the things" and so on. By the time he got through I felt overwhelmed. No wonder individualists are having a tough time in Russia. There is a huge army of bureaucrats who fear losing their jobs managing the economy. Their defense is a host of regulations, some 40 types of taxes, bribes and payoffs to discourage private enterprise. Nevertheless, Russians are starting to defy the mountain of Russian bureaucracy to establish private businesses. There are over a million small businesses today plus thousands of larger enterprises owned by shareholders.

Freedom has brought with it some lamentable problems in Russia: crime, racketeering, graft, corruption, bribery, smuggling, prostitution (sounds like home). But there are many very encouraging signs. The inflation rate has been reduced from 8,000 per cent a year to 12 per cent. And democracy is functioning. The Communists lost the 1996 election 55 per cent to 39 per cent and the Communist Party membership has fallen 90 per cent to about 500,000.

The only Communist holdouts in the world today are a reforming China (waiting for the old group to die), North Korea, Viet Nam, Cuba and, of course, the University of California at Berkeley.

The world has reason to hope that the Russian people will have the patience to endure while the reformers peel away the encrustation of over 70 years of Communist tyranny and bungling. Their patience has been tested by centuries of tyranny and mismanagement. They should be able to bear up another 30 years. And their reward should be great. The twenty-first century should be a bright one for the great people of Russia.